Self-Disclosure in Psychotherapy and Recovery

Self-Disclosure in Psychotherapy and Recovery

Gary G. Forrest, Ed.D., Ph.D.
Foreword by William Glasser, M. D.

A division of

ROWMAN & LITTLEFIELD PUBLISHERS, INC.
Lanham • Boulder • New York • Toronto • Plymouth, UK

Published by Jason Aronson
A division of Rowman & Littlefield Publishers, Inc.
A wholly owned subsidiary of The Rowman & Littlefield Publishing Group, Inc.
4501 Forbes Boulevard, Suite 200, Lanham, Maryland 20706
http://www.rowmanlittlefield.com

Estover Road
Plymouth PL6 7PY
United Kingdom

British Library Cataloguing in Publication Information Available

Library of Congress Cataloging-in-Publication Data

Forrest, Gary G.
Self-disclosure in psychotherapy and recovery / Gary G. Forrest.
p. cm.
Includes bibliographical references and index.
ISBN 978-0-7657-0726-0 (cloth : alk. paper) — ISBN 978-0-7657-0728-4 (electronic)
1. Self-disclosure. 2. Psychotherapy—Methodology. 3. Psychotherapists and patient. 4. Substance abuse—Patients—Counseling of. I. Title.
[DNLM: 1. Self Disclosure. 2. Counseling—methods. 3. Professional-Patient Relations. 4. Psychotherapy—methods. 5. Substance-Related Disorders—psychology. 6. Substance-Related Disorders—therapy. BF 697.5.S427 F728s 2009]
BF697.5.S427F67 2009
616.89'14—dc22 2009032395

Printed in the United States of America

™ The paper used in this publication meets the minimum requirements of American National Standard for Information Sciences—Permanence of Paper for Printed Library Materials, ANSI/NISO Z39.48-1992.

To Sandy, Allison, Sarah, Dr. Rob, Della,
the other "sides" of my extended family,
and my friends and patients

Contents

Foreword

Dr. Forrest has long been recognized as a pioneer in the modern era of alcoholism and chemical dependency counseling and treatment. His previous books and publications have been widely read and respected by addiction specialists as well as other therapists and behavioral health professionals.

Self-Disclosure in Psychotherapy and Recovery should be required reading for all psychotherapists and counselors. Therapists and clinicians who treat alcoholics and people with various drug problems and other addictions will especially benefit from reading this book. Dr. Forrest writes with clarity, insight, and incisive understanding of the therapeutic uses and management of therapist and client self-disclosure in effective psychotherapy relationships. As usual, he has included many clinical case studies and therapy vignettes in this work. These case studies and vignettes demonstrate a diversity of self-disclosure related therapeutic dynamics and recovery related issues.

This text presents the first in-depth and comprehensive examination of therapist and client self-disclosure in psychotherapy relationships and therapeutic work with chemically dependent people. Counselor trainees, therapists, and clinicians from diverse professional backgrounds will find this book to be stimulating, provocative, thought provoking, and helpful. Dr. Forrest shows how therapists can teach their clients to use healthy self-disclosure to improve their mental health and recoveries; I highly recommend this book.

—William Glasser, M.D.
Psychiatrist and internationally recognized author, educator, and consultant

Preface

This text examines a diversity of topics associated with therapist and client self-disclosure or transparency in counseling and psychotherapy. However, as noted in the introduction of the text, self-disclosure is certainly a topic of importance that also transcends the realm of psychotherapy and behavioral science. A plethora of issues have always been related to the self-disclosing behaviors of human beings. Politicians and business people, physicians and patients, scientists, clergy, and people from every walk of life are continually faced with questions and dilemmas associated with self-disclosing behavior. These issues are also touched upon in this book.

The introduction to this work briefly elucidates the author's historic and on-going interests in self-disclosure in psychotherapy and addictions therapy. This chapter also focuses upon some of the thorny issues pertaining to self-disclosing behaviors in business, politics, mental health care, the workplace environment, and chemical dependency treatment.

Chapter 2 provides definitions of self-disclosure in counseling and psychotherapy as well as historic perspectives on therapist or counselor self-disclosure within the context of helping relationships. Current perspectives on therapist or counselor self-disclosure in therapy are also discussed in the chapter. The author points out that therapist self-disclosure is an essential but also complicated pathway to client growth and change within the therapeutic relationship.

Chapter 3 explores historic and contemporary psychoanalytic and psychodynamically-oriented, humanistic, existential, client or person-centered, cognitive-behavioral, family and marital, group, and mechanistic therapist theoretical orientations and approaches to self-disclosure in therapy.

Therapist self-disclosing behavior exists on a continuum and often varies according to the therapist's theoretical orientation to counseling and therapy. Humanistic, existential, and client-centered therapists tend to be very open, disclosing, and authentic in their therapeutic relationships. Cognitive-behavioral therapists are generally far less self-disclosing, and mechanistic therapists tend to be least disclosing in their treatment relationships. Many chemical dependency counselors are very self-disclosing in their counseling relationships; however, counselors and therapists from any school or theoretical model of therapy may vary considerably with regard to personal self-disclosure style.

The fourth chapter addresses the effects of therapist and patient or client self-disclosure in psychotherapy. Therapist self-disclosures tend to be viewed as favorable by clients and result in more client self-disclosures in therapy. Therapist self-disclosures also foster client insight, feelings of improvement, and reinforce client disclosures and honesty in therapy. However, studies also indicate that therapist self-disclosures can produce mixed or even negative effects in therapy.

Patients and clients who are more open and self-disclosing early in the therapeutic relationship tend to have better therapeutic outcomes than non-disclosing clients. Low disclosing psychiatric patients also exhibit more severe psychopathology than high disclosing psychiatric patients, and high disclosing alcoholic patients more often tend to actively engage in the treatment process and evidence better treatment outcomes than low disclosing alcoholic patients.

Therapist and client self-disclosures always have the potential to sicken the self, other, or therapeutic alliance as well as other human relationships. Protracted therapist exposure to client self-disclosures can prove upsetting and toxic to all therapists; however, therapists and counselors always need to remain vigilant and focused in their efforts to utilize appropriate and therapeutically efficacious self-disclosures in their work with conflicted persons.

Ethical issues associated with therapist self-disclosure in psychotherapy are examined in chapter 5. Definitions and parameters of professional ethical behavior are elucidated in this chapter as well as American Psychological Association (APA) ethical standards that pertain to therapist self-disclosure in therapy. Peterson (2002) reports that the self-disclosure literature suggests that therapist self-disclosure is often ethically appropriate and may also be ethically necessary.

A number of the ethical dilemmas pertaining to chemical dependency counselors and the addictions treatment field are also addressed in chapter 5. The author noted that many addictions counselors and especially recovering counselors may tend to overutilize personal self-disclosures as a therapeutic tool. As noted in the chapter, clinicians manifest a diversity of opinions, practices, and often conflicting viewpoints pertaining to the ethics of therapist self-disclosure in psychotherapy. The author encourages all counselors and therapists to aspire to maintain an ethical level of practice which transcends the minimal rules and standards of their professions.

Chapter 6 focuses upon the various facets of self-disclosure, addiction, and the recovery process. The various roles and dynamics of self-disclosing behavior in the etiology and maintenance of addictive disorders, the impact of self-disclosure on the recovery process, therapist and client self-disclosure in addictions psychotherapy, self-disclosure and the Alcoholics Anonymous (AA) self-help recovery model (Adams, 2009), and self-disclosure and recovery from severe psychological problems and even major psychiatric illness are topics that are examined in this chapter. The chapter also includes case studies involving a compulsive gambler, compulsive overeater, and an alcohol-dependent person.

The relevance, importance, and various dynamics of self-disclosure in recovery from a diversity of addictions and substance abuse disorders, psychological problems, and psychiatric disorders constitute the essence of this chapter. Self-disclosure plays a multiplicity of roles in the development and maintenance of all these human problems.

Chapter 7 is limited to an examination of many important therapeutic aspects of self-disclosure in the specific realm of chemical dependency counseling and addictions treatment. Therapist and client self-disclosure related matters pertaining to etiological, diagnostic and assessment, therapeutic process, iatrogenic disclosures, and treatment effectiveness and efficacy are considered in this chapter. Several brief case studies as well as actual therapy vignettes are also included in the chapter. These case studies demonstrate the different therapeutic dynamics of self-disclosure in chemical dependency therapy.

Client and counselor self-disclosure to self and self-disclosure as a mechanism of confession are also briefly discussed in the chapter.

Chapter 8 includes several client and professional therapist perspectives on self-disclosure in counseling, psychotherapy, and addictions treatment. The contributors to this chapter provide a diversity of fascinating and often divergent perspectives pertaining to self-disclosure in helping relationships. Readers will find that the perspectives of chemical dependency counselors and recovering professionals tend to be far more disclosing in nature than the perspectives of non-recovering helping professionals. Readers will find that the client perspectives in this chapter are also very revealing and transparent in nature.

This text will be especially helpful for all graduate and neophyte level counselor trainees, clinical and counseling psychologists, addiction and substance abuse counselors, social workers, family and marriage therapists, and psychiatrists. Counselors and clinicians who specialize in addictions and substance abuse treatment will benefit greatly via the ideas, content, practice, and research material that is presented in this book. Readers will become much more cognizant of the relevance and complexity of self-disclosure in all helping relationships as they read the text.

The self-disclosure dynamism impacts every facet of our social, intrapersonal, affective, and cognitive interactions. Psychotherapy and other forms of intimate human relationships are especially impacted by self-disclosure. Self-disclosure transactions can always be "for better or worse" in nature. As noted frequently throughout this text, nondisclosing behaviors as well as self-disclosures based upon lies and dishonesty consistently accompany a diversity of dysfunctional adjustment styles and contribute significantly to poor counseling and psychotherapy outcomes. Healthy self-disclosing behaviors are one *sine qua non* of optimal human adjustment as well as efficacious psychotherapy relationships with a diversity of patient populations.

Effective psychotherapists consistently employ a diversity of self-disclosure and transparency-based techniques to teach their clients more appropriate and healthy self-disclosing behaviors. The majority of research evidence (Farber, 2006, 2009; Farber and Sohn, 2007) points to a positive but somewhat complex association between client and therapist self-disclosure in psychotherapy and therapeutic outcomes. However, therapeutic disclosures of information should always involve values that are central to the ethical and professional guidelines of the behavioral health and psychotherapy professions (Behnke, 2007). Values and the process for determining whether a disclosure is appropriate are established via a professional ethics code.

Acknowledgments

Many people have provided a diversity of contributions to this book. As always, my family and extended family has been supportive and encouraging—especially my wife, Sandy; our daughters, Sarah and Allison; granddaughter, Della; and my son-in-law, Rob Ochsner, M.D. My clients have continually provided the educational and relational nexus essential to my continued publications over the past thirty-five years. I must also thank my "new" typist, Laura Price, for bringing the text to fruition. A very special thanks to Mary DeShong for completing the final touches to this work, and June Miller for her support as our office manager over the past decade. Finally, my continued collegial relationships with L.E. Wellman, Ed.D., Dennis Caldwell, M.D., Barb Martin, LCSW, Mike Wilbourn, Psy.D., William Glasser, M.D., and numerous others in the addictions treatment and behavioral health fields have simply sustained and nurtured me over all these years. My work and career have rarely been easy, but the support, love, joy, and encouragement of others has always propelled and sustained my continued efforts.

Chapter 1

Introduction

Throughout the course of some thirty-five years as a practicing clinical psychologist and psychotherapist, I have never ceased to be interested in the various facets of self-disclosure in psychotherapy. My professional interests in self-disclosure began with my first doctoral dissertation, "Transparency as a Prognostic Variable in Psychotherapy" (Forrest, 1970), and has been continued in one fashion or another via numerous subsequent books and publications. As I approach the end of my professional career as a clinical psychologist and practicing therapist, I am just as fascinated and intrigued with the various facets of self-disclosure or transparency in psychotherapy as I was as a young doctoral student.

Self-disclosure is a topic of importance that also transcends the realm of counseling and psychotherapy. Human beings are continuously confronted with the moment-to-moment choice of revealing or not revealing who they are, expressing or not expressing their real feelings and thoughts, masking their true beliefs, or attempting to be seen as something they are not. Throughout history, human beings have often chosen to conceal their real or authentic being behind various masks and roles. Human beings often deny, repress, conceal, and camouflage their true being in order to feel safe and avoid criticism, hurt, or rejection. And yet, paradoxically, when we are not authentically known by the other people in our lives, we can only be misunderstood. As we become progressively more successful at hiding and denying our authentic being from others, we tend to lose touch with our own inner being and real selves. This loss of real self may contribute to various forms of illness and non-well being. At the very least, this process can erode our basic sense of humanness.

Modern politicians and businessmen are notoriously adept at covering up and masking their feelings and true thoughts, and not disclosing the real facts associated with their business dealings and lives. Their disclosures may be dishonest or based on "half-truths." Millions of Americans have recently become the victims of corporate fraud perpetuated by nondisclosing and/or dishonestly disclosing CEOs, CFOs, accounting firms, and other upper-level management personnel. Little wonder that these captains of modern industry choose to hide and cover up their authentic identities rather than openly disclose and reveal themselves! Self-concealment continues to be regarded by many, if not most, men as a natural state of behavior and being. And yet, these very forms of nondisclosure and dishonest self-disclosure adversely impact all of our lives.

The partial self-disclosures, dishonest self-disclosures, and basic lack of self-disclosure upon the part of President Clinton not only cost American taxpayers millions of dollars, but proved to be costly in myriad ways and destructive to countless numbers of people including President Clinton and his family as well as Monica Lewinski and her family. The Catholic Church seems to perpetually be in the midst of a "crisis" centered around the matters of disclosure and nondisclosure. A significant number of priests, bishops, and other clergy have been involved in the sexual abuse of children and parishioners for decades and probably forever. And this matter is certainly not limited to the Catholic Church. The perpetrators of these horrendous acts have not been open and self-disclosing about their behaviors, thoughts and impulses, or feelings. Nor have their supervisors and superiors been open and disclosing about these matters. Churches have historically attempted to deny and cover up their dark histories. How many millions of people have been damaged or destroyed by these malignant transactions over the years? How many billions of dollars have been paid to attorneys, law firms, and victims by the Catholic Church in recent years?

Pedophiles and child sex abusers are especially adept at denying, covering up, and minimizing the destructive nature of their acts. Sex offenders will go to any lengths to avoid disclosing their behavior and even when caught and incarcerated, they have an uncanny ability to deny and rationalize their behaviors.

The victims of childhood sexual abuse have also historically been closed, guarded, and non–self-disclosing about their abuse and trauma (Boriskin, 2009). Surprisingly, a large number of people who have been the victims of financial scams or corporate financial corruption also don't want to openly discuss or share these painful experiences with others. It can be extremely difficult to even self-admit or self-disclose these painful realities. Victims of these transactions tend to feel embarrassed, perhaps believe that "it" is their fault, or somehow believe their stupidity caused them to get what "they deserved."

While large numbers of people in America and through out the world are beginning to change these patterns of non-disclosing behavior, I continuously interact with many people who do not want their family members, friends, or neighbors to know that they have been diagnosed with cancer or have some other difficult medical condition. A few of my psychotherapy patients choose not to tell their spouses or family that they have a terminal illness. And the stigma of alcoholism, drug abuse, depression, and mental illness is still very much alive and well! Trust me on that one. A good friend finally asked me for some guidance and help with his son a few years ago. He approached me and disclosed the turmoil and pain in his life after months of drug addiction, legal entanglements, and out of control psychotic behaviors on the part of his son. A few years later and with therapy, family concern, support and love, appropriate medication, and a lot of hard work, my friend's son is a true miracle in every sense of the word: a recent college graduate, a business executive, a married man, and a responsible, taxpaying American citizen. And he even has a great sense of humor!

Chemically dependent persons are notoriously the last people to disclose that they have "a problem." These individuals never really disclose their chemical dependency to themselves or others while they are actively addicted. They seem to be incapable of authentically and openly disclosing or acknowledging their addiction unless they are drunk or under the influence of drugs, or after they become drug free and committed to some form of real treatment and the recovery process. Millions of chemically dependent persons continue to deny their addictive disorders or disease to the point of death. Denying and dying are the antithesis of self-disclosing, growing, and optimally living.

Just as most people are able to eventually recognize the insanity, destruction, and pathology associated with the lack of honesty and authentic self-disclosures upon the part of pedophiles or psychopathic "leaders" such as Adolph Hitler, Osama Bin-Laden, Sadam Hussein, Stalin, Herman Goering, or Zarkowi, every person who is intimately or even tangentially involved with an actively chemically dependent person also eventually begins to comprehend the insane and destructive nature of the addicted person's pathological lack of authentic self-disclosure.

The pathology of chemical dependency is progressive and evolutional. Self-disclosure is an important and multidimensional facet of both the evolving addiction process and the evolving recovery process. The disclosing style of chemically dependent persons in the early stages of counseling and psychotherapy is generally quite different from the self-disclosing behaviors these individuals exude later in the therapeutic process (Forrest, 1997, 2009). The self-disclosing behavior of many, if not most, chemically dependent persons who have sustained several years of drug abstinence and remained active in some form of on-going recovery program is based upon the precept of "rigorous honesty." The self-disclosures of these individuals are consciously and consistently genuine, factual, accurate, and sometimes brutally honest. Unlike the self-disclosures of the chemically dependent client who shows up for an initial early stage therapy session acutely intoxicated and reports that he or she has had "nothing to drink" or perhaps reportedly consumed "a couple of drinks," the self-disclosing style of the genuinely recovering client is based upon truth, "reality," and honesty. At times, the self-disclosing style of the actively chemically dependent person is as overtly bizarre, dishonest, and non-reality oriented as the disclosures of "Baghdad Bob," who many of us remember watching on national television during the early days of the second Iraq war!

There are also a multiplicity of caveats and paradoxes associated with self-disclosure in the realms of general social interaction, psychotherapy, and mental health. Self-disclosure or transparency is not in any way an "all or none" or absolute matter in any form of human interaction or communication. As I was beginning the process of working on this book during an extended beach vacation in South Carolina, a sister-in-law disclosed a very personal and current matter pertaining to her extended history of relational difficulties with men. I then chose to disclose this information to my wife and also shared my related concerns about our daughter taking a brief trip with my sister-in-law. The decision to disclose these matters to my wife evolved into an upsetting brief family "fire storm." I had originally shared with my sister-in-law that I did not want to discuss the original matter, which she had eventually pressured me to hear out, and then I regretted having disclosed this information to my wife, and I most definitely regretted that she further disclosed this matter to her sister as well as our daughter! Self-disclosure and openness in the family system is but one of many social arenas where there are many sources of risk and conflict as well as growth, change, and potential benefit associated with this form of behavior.

How many employees have lost their jobs over the past few years as a result of being "whistle blowers?" In essence, a "whistle blower" is a person in the work environment who chooses to disclose information that is somehow damaging or potentially damaging to the company, business organization, or select individuals in an organizational system. Scientists and researchers at NASA who attempted to share their concerns about structural problems or faulty heat shield tiles on space shuttle aircraft or related matters and then made their efforts known to the public following a "shuttle disaster" no doubt paid a price for their honesty and self-disclosing behavior. A British scientist who had previously been involved in the Iraq inspections for biological, chemical, and nuclear weapons of mass destruction committed suicide. Apparently this tragic event was triggered in some part as a result of the attempted disclosures the scientist made pertaining to Great Britain's handling of the information. And self-disclosure in any correctional environment can be tantamount to any number of destructive consequences including a death sentence by other inmates. After all, a "snitch" is perhaps nothing more than a disclosing or self-disclosing person in a correctional facility. At the same time, "con men" often use their self-disclosing tactics to destructively scam millions of unsuspecting persons every day in every city and country in the world.

Several years ago an alcoholic patient came to my office with a loaded 45-caliber pistol and informed me of his intent to leave my office and go directly to the office of the post command sergeant major, and kill the sergeant major. The sergeant major had been sexually involved with his wife for several months. I attempted to get the patient to give me his pistol and rather frantically tried to use a number of cognitive-behavioral interventions to basically talk the patient out of his decision to kill the sergeant major. My efforts failed within a matter of minutes, and the patient left my office with his gun, intent on carrying out his plan. I immediately called the military police and the chief of psychiatry and reported the circumstances of this situation. The patient was arrested a few blocks from my office and immediately hospitalized at a local civilian psychiatric facility for several weeks. Within a day or two, "Mr. Earl" began calling me one or two times a day, telling me that he was going to kill *me* as soon as he was discharged from the hospital. He repeatedly threatened to kill me because I had betrayed him. I had "disclosed" his plan to the police and authorities. After a number of days, I did go to the hospital and met with Mr. Earl and attempted to rationally discuss my personal, professional, and legal obligations in this difficult situation. He was discharged from the hospital several weeks later, and I never heard from him again. Thank God, no one was killed or injured in this situation.

The paradoxical nature of self-disclosing via psychotherapy and professional clinical practice is perhaps even better exemplified by the case of a psychologist in a southern state who was recently sued for approximately one million dollars and *lost* in a duty-to-warn case. During the course of completing a neuropsychological evaluation or therapy session, the psychologist learned of his patient's intent to kill or harm a specific person and, as required by his professional ethical code in the state where he practiced, then notified the potential victim of the possible imminent danger he was facing. The psychologist's patient did not harm or kill the potential victim in this case. Eventually, the patient sued the psychologist for breach of confidentiality and won! Due to the "damned if you do, damned if you don't" nature of the duty-to-warn statute (Lane, 2006) and the myriad difficulties associated with the clinical prediction of violence or harm to self/others, Texas has recently abolished the mental health professionals' duty to warn in these types of situations.

This book examines the complex and nefarious issues associated with self-disclosure in psychotherapy, chemical dependency counseling, the self-help community, and the recovery process. Many core issues that are germane to the more general topics of self-disclosure, counseling and psychotherapy, chemical dependency counseling, and the recovery process are discussed throughout the book. Psychotherapists and chemical dependency counselors will benefit greatly from this broader examination of self-disclosure within the context of their helping relationships.

Definitions of self-disclosure and a general discussion of the historical as well as current perspectives on self-disclosure are included in chapter 2. Chapter 3 examines the impact of therapist theoretical orientation on self-disclosure. The effects of therapist and client self-disclosure in psychotherapy are discussed in chapter 4. Ethical perspectives on therapist self-disclosure are examined in chapter 5. Chapter 6 addresses self-disclosure, addiction, and the recovery process, and chapter 7 examines self-disclosure in chemical dependency counseling. Client and therapist perspectives on self-disclosure and recovery are presented in chapter 8. The final chapter summarizes core ideas, research and clinical findings, and other material presented throughout the text.

As Jourard (1964) noted many years ago, "no man can come to know himself except as an outcome of disclosing himself to another person." However, Jourard also stated while commenting on self-disclosure and general mental health, "I have some evidence that the relationship between the two variables is curvilinear . . . too much or too little self-disclosure betokens disturbance in self and in interpersonal relationships, while as yet an undetermined amount under specified conditions is synonymous with mental health . . . self-disclosure is the obverse of repression and self-alienation" (p. 15).

The reader will discover that Jourard's (1964, 1967) general perspectives on self-disclosure are congruent with many of our contemporary beliefs, research findings, and clinical viewpoints on self-disclosure in psychotherapy, chemical dependency counseling, and recovery.

It is my hope that this short text will be heuristic as well as educational, and especially beneficial for graduate level counseling and clinical psychology students, counselor educators and supervisors, and all psychotherapists and chemical dependency counselors. Education, training, self-awareness, and self-disclosure (Forrest, 2002, 2006; Halbur and Halbur, 2006; Kasper, Hill and Kivlighan, 2008) are some of the basic precursors to therapist growth, change, and enhanced self- and treatment-related efficacy.

Chapter 2

Self-Disclosure in Counseling and Psychotherapy

INTRODUCTION

Counselors and psychotherapists are quite simply human beings and subject to the entire gamut of human experiences. Many or most of the experiences of therapists and counselors are pleasant, fun, rewarding, and enjoyable. Like all humans, counselors also experience periodic emotional pain, physical illness, loss, career shifts, family and relational struggles, financial insecurities, and eventually death. However, unlike most other professionals who experience all of these potentially disturbing life events, counselors and therapists are continuously forced to deal with the entire gamut of both personal and client experiences, emotions, struggles, and needs associated with the various processes of living.

While all counselors engage in various forms of self-disclosure in their relationships with clients, considerable professional controversy and disagreement surrounds issues pertaining to "what, where, and when or even how or if" counselors and therapists should self-disclose within the context of their counseling and psychotherapeutic relationships (Farber, 2006).

This chapter examines the definitional parameters of counselor self-disclosure in counseling and psychotherapy, historical perspectives on counselor self-disclosure within the helping relationship, and current perspectives on the uses, reasons, and rationale for counselor self-disclosure in counseling and psychotherapy.

DEFINING THERAPIST OR COUNSELOR SELF-DISCLOSURE IN COUNSELING AND PSYCHOTHERAPY

Cashwell, Shcherbakova, and Cashwell (2003) define counselor self-disclosure as the "verbal sharings by the counselor of personal revelations or information to the client" (p. 196). These authors go on to indicate that counselor self-disclosure has been identified as a key process variable in the counseling relationship and then emphasize that "self-disclosing statements by a counselor should be distinguished from "*self-involving*" statements. The former refer to personal factual information about the counselor, whereas the latter involves the disclosure of counselor cognitions and emotions related to the client" (p. 196).

These authors (Cashwell, Shcherbakova, and Caswell, 2003) go on to indicate that empirical research has consistently supported the efficacy of counselor self-involving statements in the counseling relationship, but research on self-disclosing statements has produced variable results, sometimes supporting the efficacy of self-disclosure and at other times demonstrating no relationship. Cashwell, et al. (2003) also indicate "in the specific case of disclosing sexual attraction to clients, counselor disclosure actually decreased perceived counselor expertness and the therapeutic quality of the session, although disclosing counselors were viewed as more likeable, warm, and accepting" (p. 196).

One of the more consistent findings in the self-disclosure research is that self-disclosing counselors are seen as more attractive than nondisclosing counselors (Goodyear and Shumate, 1996). Counselor attractiveness is a component of the social influence model of counseling and refers to characteristics such as warmth, acceptance, and likeability (Cashwell et al., 2003).

According to Hill and Knox (2001), therapist self-disclosure can be broadly defined as "statements that reveal something personal about therapists" (p. 413). These authors (Hill and Knox, 2001) go on to indicate that although most of the literature has used this broad definition, it is "important to distinguish self-disclosures which reveal non-immediate personal information from immediacy statements. The latter reveal immediate feelings about the client or the therapeutic relationship" (p. 414). "Immediacy statements" would also no doubt include the therapist's expressions of immediate feelings or cognitions about himself or herself. Hill and Knox (2001) also note that therapist self-disclosure is "one of the most controversial therapist interventions, with some therapists enthusiastically promoting it and others adamantly opposing its use" (p. 413). Importantly, these authors go on to report that most of the existing research pertaining to therapist self-disclosure has been analogue in design (i.e., studies employing simulated therapy sessions and situations and involving graduate students rather than actual therapy sessions involving therapists and patients).

Bridges (2001) defines *intentional self-disclosure* as "a valuable tool in a therapeutic relationship that facilitates exploration, introduces new perspectives on the self in relationships, and conveys to the patient the possibility of creating a new, healing object relationship" (p. 22). This author (Bridges, 2001) also indicates that intentional self-disclosure "opens up space for deep therapeutic engagement between therapist and patient. It heightens self-perception, affective experience, and relational connection" (p. 21). Self-disclosure is not only an inevitable component of the therapeutic relationship, but also an essential ingredient in the counseling or psychotherapeutic process according to this author. She also indicates that self-disclosure is an "inevitable integral, and essential therapeutic tool" (Bridges, 2001).

Self-disclosure (Peterson, 2002) has been defined broadly "as a process by which the therapist reveals aspects of himself or herself to the client" (p. 21). Peterson (2002) also states that "avoiding all forms of self-disclosure is impossible . . . After all, the therapist's gender, ethnicity, style of dress, office decorations, and involvement in public activities all expose information about the therapist's self" (p. 21). This author correctly indicates that most publications dealing with therapist self-disclosure focus primarily upon the various clinical issues related to this topic.

In summary, recent definitions (Farber, 2006; Farber, Khurgin-Bott and Feldman, 2009; Roes, 2004) of self-disclosure in counseling and psychotherapy emphasize the counselor or therapist's verbal sharing with the client of personal information and the process whereby the therapist openly reveals various aspects of himself or herself to the client. Several authors (Bridges, 2001; Cashwell, et. al., 2003; Hill and Knox, 2001) also distinguish between counselor self-disclosures that reveal personal factual information about the counselor and counselor self-disclosures that reveal the counselor's personal feelings and thoughts about the client, himself or herself, and the therapeutic relationship. Counselor self-disclosure or authenticity (Forrest, 1997) can also include the counselor's open discussion of personal life experiences or, in the broadest definitional sense, sharing any aspect of the self with the client. Most definitions of self-disclosure directly or inferentially refer to the intentional, thought-out, conscious, and purposeful nature of therapist self-disclosures. However, spontaneous self-disclosures may also occur at any juncture in the therapeutic process. Therapeutic self-disclosures may also reflect pre-conscious and unconscious processes.

Finally, it is important to indicate (Hill and Knox, 2001; Hill, Stahl and Roffman, 2007) that many different definitions of therapist self-disclosure have been used in the empirical and clinical literature. Clinicians and researchers need to clearly define what they mean by counselor or therapist self-disclosure, and subtypes of self-disclosure also need to be clearly delineated.

HISTORICAL PERSPECTIVES ON THERAPIST SELF-DISCLOSURE IN COUNSELING AND PSYCHOTHERAPY

Sidney M. Jourard (1964, 1968) was one of the earliest and most prolific writers, researchers, and therapists to explore a diversity of issues associated with self-disclosure in counseling and psychotherapy as well as the basic context of human interaction. He (Jourard, 1964) defined self-disclosure as "letting another person know what you think, feel, or want is the most direct means (though not the only means) by which an individual can make himself known to another person . . . an operational analysis of what goes on in counseling and therapy shows that the patients and clients discover themselves through self-disclosure to the counselor" (p. 24). Identifying self-disclosure as "a factor in the process of effective counseling and psychotherapy," Jourard (1964) further suggests that "people become clients because they have not yet disclosed themselves in some optimum degree to the people in their life" (p. 21). This author (Jourard, 1958) indicates that "real" self-disclosure is both a symptom of personality health and at the same time a means for ultimately achieving healthy personality. He goes on to say "it is not until I am my real self and I act my real self that my real self is in a position to grow. One's self grows from the consequence of being" (p. 25).

Jourard (1964) believed that "every maladjusted person is a person who has not made himself known to another human being and in consequence does not know himself. Nor can he be himself more than that, if he struggles actively to avoid becoming known by another human being" (p. 21). Interestingly, Jourard also indicates that the greater the discrepancy between the unexpurgated real self and the version on a person's self that is presented to others, then the more dangerous will other people be for the individual. For Jourard (1964), full disclosure of the self to at least one other significant human being "appears to be one means by which a person discovers not only the breadth and depth of his needs and feelings, but also the nature of his own self-affirmed values . . . real self-being is a necessary but not a sufficient condition for healthy personality" (p. 27). Jourard concurs with Rogers (1958) that love provides the optimum conditions under which man will "disclose or expose his naked, quivering self to our gaze."

The manner of the therapist's being when in the presence of the client fosters growth and change upon the part of the client, not the techniques or theoretical orientation of the therapist. Jourard (1964) states,

> Effective therapists seem to follow this implicit hypothesis: If they are themselves in the presence of the patient, avoiding compulsions to silence, to reflection, to interpretation, to impersonal technique, and kindred character disorders, but instead are striving to know their patient, involving themselves in his situation, and then responding to his utterances with their spontaneous selves, this fosters growth . . . in short, they love their patients. They employ their powers in the service of their patient's well-being and growth, not inflict them on him. Somehow there is a difference. (p. 62)

Further, the "loving therapist is quite free and spontaneous in his relationships: his responses are bound only by his ethics and his judgment. He may laugh, scold, become angry, give advice . . . in short breaking most of the rules laid down in psychotherapy training manuals . . . evidently it is only the therapist's good will which needs to be predictable, not his specific responses to a patient's disclosures" (p. 62). In short, client growth and change is fostered when the counselor is a rather free individual who functions as a person with all of his or her feelings, thoughts, and being.

Jourard (1964) further concludes: (1) the closest therapists can come to eliciting and reinforcing real-self behavior in their clients is by manifesting real-self behavior themselves, (2) when therapists are committed to the task of helping clients grow, they function as whole persons, not as disembodied intellects, computers, or reinforcement programmers, (3) in the presence of a man or woman who is of good will, even the most defensive will self-disclose, (4) no patient can be expected to drop all his or her defenses or fully disclose or reveal himself or herself *except* in the presence of someone whom he or she believes is for them, (5) therapy proceeds through *honest* responses between the client and counselor, (6) to be transparent to the client, to have nothing of one's experience in the relationship that is hidden, is basic to effective psychotherapy, (7) if a therapist hides his being from the client, he is engaging in the same behavior that generated symptoms in the client, (8) therapist openness serves gradually to relieve the client's distrust, (9) by being open and letting themselves *be* in the therapy relationship and also letting clients be, therapists provide clients with a role-model for personal growth, and (10) a therapeutic relationship can change the therapist as much as it does the client.

Early empirical investigations of self-disclosure in counseling and psychotherapy (Forrest, 1970; Hountras and Forrest, 1970) found that the initial level of client self-disclosure or transparency was not a predictor of brief-therapy outcome. However, these authors did find that low self-disclosure was related to client psychopathology within a psychiatric outpatient population. Low disclosing patients were significantly more disturbed on the MMPI clinical scales (Hountras and Forrest, 1970) than were high disclosing patients. Evidence from these investigations also suggested that extremely low self-disclosing patients and extremely high self-disclosing patients exhibited more severe psychological symptoms on the MMPI than more moderately disclosing patients.

One of the most systematic and comprehensive investigations into the process and outcome of psychotherapy ever conducted was completed between the late 1960s and early 1970s by Truax and Carkhuff (1967). These authors published a few hundred empirical investigations as well as several text books that focused upon therapist characteristics and qualities that positively and negatively impact the process and outcome of counseling and psychotherapy relationships. In a convincing summary of this research, Truax and Carkhuff (1967) identify three essential therapist ingredients in the effective psychotherapeutic relationship: accurate empathetic understanding of the patient, nonpossessive warmth, and therapist genuineness or authenticity. Therapists who consistently respond to their patients with high levels of these facilitative conditions (Forrest, 1978) "tend to help effect significant positive behavioral change and personality growth upon the part of their patients. Therapists who are unable to provide adequate levels of these facilitative conditions have been shown to consistently produce minimal or even negative therapeutic results" (p. 80).

With regard to these essential ingredients in successful therapy, therapist genuineness or authenticity (Forrest, 1997; Halbur and Halbur, 2006) is felt to be most fundamental. Genuineness (Forrest, 1978) has been defined as "the therapist's ability to be open to his or her own experience within the therapeutic encounter and to honestly express these feelings to the patient" (p. 80). More simply, the therapist is a real person; he or she wears no façade, expresses feelings and experiences to the patient within the therapeutic encounter, and makes every attempt to relate in a personally relevant manner within this context (Truax and Lister, 1971; Truax and Wargo, 1966). Self-disclosure is essential to therapist genuineness (Forrest, 1992 and 2009; Halbur and Halbur, 2006).

Truax and Carkhuff (1967) also report that as early as the second interview, level of patient self-disclosure can provide a reasonably adequate prediction of final therapy outcome.

A number of empirical and clinical studies pertaining to counselor or therapist self-disclosure have been published over the past three decades (Farber, 2006; Farber and Sohn, 2007). These investigations have addressed such diverse topics as the effects of sex and intimacy on levels of self-disclosure (DeForest and Stone, 1980; Farber, Khurgin-Bott and Feldman, 2009), differential effects of counselor self-disclosure, self-involving statements, and interpretation (Dowd and Boroto, 1982), self-disclosure flexibility and counselor effectiveness (Neimeyer and Fong, 1983), effect of paradoxical and nonparadoxical self-disclosure on counselor social influence (Perrin and Dowd, 1986), why self-disclosing counselors are attractive (Peca-Baker and Friedlander, 1989), research effects of counselor self-disclosure (Watkins, 1990), characteristics of therapist self-disclosure in the counseling process, self-disclosure in treatment, what therapists do and don't talk about (Goldstein, 1994), and psychodynamic psychotherapy, religious beliefs, and self disclosure (Tillman, 1998).

It is very apparent that counselors and therapists as well as other behavioral scientists continue to be very interested in a wide diversity of issues related to counselor self-disclosure.

CURRENT PERSPECTIVES ON THERAPIST SELF-DISCLOSURE IN COUNSELING AND PSYCHOTHERAPY

Several research studies indicate that therapist self-disclosure occurs rather infrequently in the context of individual psychotherapy (Barkham and Shapiro, 1986; Farber, 2006; Hill and Knox, 2001; Hill, Thames and Rardin, 1979; Stiles, Shapiro and Firth-Cozens, 1988; Roes, 2004). These investigations report that "1 to 13% (mean of 3.5% across studies) of all therapist interventions in individual therapy were self-disclosures" (Hill and Knox, 2001).

Therapists and counselors most frequently self-disclose about their professional backgrounds (education, training, therapy style, and orientation) and least frequently about their sexual behavior and beliefs (Edwards and Murdock, 1994; Geller and Farber, 1997). Counselor self-disclosures tend not to involve intimate personal experiences and behaviors. It should be noted that many state licensure laws require psychologists, counselors, addictions counselors, social workers, and other behavioral health professionals to disclose information pertaining to several personal and professional issues (i.e., education, licensure, theoretical orientation, statement about inappropriateness and unethical nature of any form of sexual involvement between counselors and clients, etc.). Furthermore, several states require counselors, psychologists, and mental health workers and addiction specialists to provide clients a written professional disclosure statement.

Studies (Edwards and Murdock, 1994; Robitschek and McCarthy, 1991) report no differences in self-disclosure between male and female therapists nor among counselors and therapists of different racial or ethnic background. However, Cashwell et al. (2003) found that African American clients indicated a stronger preference for counselor self-disclosure in the areas of personal feelings, sexual issues, and professional successes and failures than did Caucasian clients. These preferences occurred regardless of the ethnicity of the counselor. It should also be noted that this study (Cashwell et al., 2003) involved a nonclinical sample.

Wells (1994) defined several categories of therapist self-disclosure. These categories include: (1) information about the therapist's training and practice, (2) information about personal life experiences, circumstances, and attitudes, (3) personal reactions to the client and personal feelings about the client, and (4) admissions of therapist mistakes in therapy.

The matter of why counselors and therapists self-disclose is especially germane to any discussion of self-disclosure in counseling and psychotherapy. Hill et al. (1988) indicated that therapists disclose to provide information to clients and not to resolve their own needs. Survey data (Edwards and Murdock, 1994; Geller and Farber, 1997; Simon, 1990) reveals that therapists often disclose to "increase perceived similarity between themselves and their clients, model appropriate behavior for clients, foster the therapeutic alliance, validate reality or normalize client experiences, offer alternative ways of thinking and acting, and satisfy clients who wanted therapist disclosure (Hill and Knox, 2001)" (p. 414).

Goldstein (1997) stressed the importance of self-disclosing for empathetic reasons rather than selfish reasons. Curtis and Hodge (1994) indicate that self-disclosure can be used by mental health workers to (1) establish bonds of trust and understanding, (2) normalize client feelings, experiences, and concerns, (3) teach and model behavior and coping skills, and 4) demonstrate effective emoting skills. These authors (Curtis and Hodge, 1994) also indicate that mental health workers who refuse to disclose personal information and experiences act in a manner that suggests they have no feelings or problems, which in turn undermines one of the most useful aspects of the counseling relationship. Promoting feelings of universality, fostering client self-disclosure, promoting the importance of the client-counselor relationship, and decreasing client rigidity have also been identified as reasons for counselor self-disclosure (Mahalik et al., 2000). Self-disclosure may help clients feel more comfortable and relaxed and less anxious or stressed within the context of the therapeutic relationship.

Cooper (1998) delineated three therapeutic purposes of therapist self-disclosure: (1) converting unconscious transference content to a conscious level, (2) facilitating a new or different mode of inquiry and discovery, and (3) helping the client understand that the therapist is, or could become, a potential new relational object.

Disclosure of the analyst's emotional responses to a patient may help the patient better understand and master affective regulation as well as contribute to the patient's capacity to see himself or herself as others do (Maroda, 1999).

Counselor countertransference disclosure (Dalenberg, 2004; Forrest, 2002; Maroda, 1991; Tansey and Burke, 1989) can be utilized to confront clients with the various realities of their irresponsible behavior, narcissism, substance abuse, and relational difficulties. Contertransference disclosures can also be used as a tool for resolving therapeutic impasses, teaching clients about feelings, enhancing self-esteem, reinforcing various forms of adaptive behavior, facilitating the treatment and recovery process, and enhancing both therapist and client awareness pertaining to the state of the counseling relationship. The therapist's disclosure of countertransference material may also deepen the client's capacity for insight, foster relational attachment to the therapist, and enhance the therapeutic alliance. However, countertransference disclosure (Forrest, 2002) is also especially fraught with potential risks and complications associated with timing, content, and the unpredictable impact of these disclosures upon the client as well as the counseling relationship.

Counselors and therapists (Farber, Khurgin-Bott and Feldman, 2009; Forrest, 2005; Roes, 2004) need to exercise caution and forethought when self-disclosing in the counseling relationship. Thus, therapist self-disclosure can be a risky therapeutic intervention. When should therapists not disclose? Hill and Knox (2001) report that therapists "generally avoided self-disclosure when the disclosure was for their own needs or when the disclosure would move the focus from the client to the therapist, would interfere with the client's flow of material, would burden or confuse the client, would be intrusive for the client, would blur boundaries between the therapist and client, would over-stimulate the client, or would contaminate the transference" (p. 414). Bridges (2001) adds, "therapists employing intentional self-disclosure are advised to remain patient focused, rely upon the patient's resources and expertise, model emotional honesty, and share their view of the clinical situation at hand. Exploration of the multiple interpersonal and intrapsychic meanings of the disclosure to the patient and the treatment process is essential" (p. 23). She also implores clinicians to use continuous self-scrutiny throughout the clinical process and notes that patients report a broad range of feelings about therapist self-disclosures and their impact upon the therapeutic relationship.

Most therapists and counselors experience ambivalence about self-disclosing to their clients, and a few clinicians may feel extremely vulnerable when they use this therapeutic tool. Bridges (2001) astutely observes "a willingness to intentionally disclose and share your view in therapeutic relationships means allowing your patients to see you, to know you, and to engage in what may feel like a personal conversation that has a therapeutic intent and purpose . . . As therapists reveal feelings and aspects of themselves they, too, feel vulnerable and exposed to the scrutiny of patients" (p. 25). In reality, counselors and clients continually self-disclose and self-reveal in counseling and psychotherapy relationships and these transactions often (1) provoke mutual anxiety, (2) stir discomfort upon the part of one of the participants, or (3) cause disequilibrium within the therapeutic alliance. And yet, the mutually self-disclosing dialogue and interaction between counselor and client constitutes the communicative and relational nexus for constructive growth and change upon the part of both participants.

It is simply impossible to know in advance (Farber, Khurgin-Bott and Feldman, 2009) how the therapist's or the client's self-disclosures will impact the therapist, client, therapeutic relationship, or the treatment process.

On the basis of research evidence pertaining to self-disclosure, Hill and Knox (2001) recommend the following therapist practice guidelines:

> (1) therapists should generally disclose infrequently, (2) the most appropriate topic for therapist self-disclosure involves professional background, whereas the least appropriate topics include sexual practices and beliefs, (3) therapists should generally use disclosures to validate reality, normalize, model, strengthen the alliance, or offer alternative ways to think or act, (4) therapists should generally avoid using disclosures that are for their own needs, remove the focus from the client, interfere with the flow of the session, burden or confuse the client, are intrusive, blur the boundaries, or over-stimulate the client, (5) therapist self-disclosure in response to similar client self-disclosure seems to be particularly effective in eliciting client self-disclosure, (6) therapists should observe carefully how clients respond to their disclosures, ask about client reactions, and use this information to conceptualize the clients and decide how to intervene next, and (7) it may be especially important for therapists to disclose with clients who have difficulty forming relationships in the therapeutic setting. (p. 416)

Counselor self-disclosure is an essential and valuable therapeutic tool in counseling and psychotherapy work. However, it is apparent that a great deal more research and clinical investigation needs to be conducted in the areas of client and counselor readiness for disclosures, specific topical content of disclosures, temporal nature of disclosures, and the relationships between client and counselor self-disclosures upon the actual process and outcome of therapy.

Self-disclosure is clearly an essential but complicated (Forrest, 2005; Freimuth, 2008; Mallinckrodt, et al., 2005; Roes, 2004) pathway to relational change, and both researchers and clinicians need to keep these realities in mind as they develop new methods of behavioral science investigation. Finally, it is important to emphasize that most of the existing research on therapist self-disclosure has relied upon analogue designs or methodology (Kahn et al., 2008). Thus, most therapist self-disclosure research evidence is based upon studies involving simulations of therapy rather than actual therapy situations.

SUMMARY

Counselor or therapist self-disclosure generally refers to the process of verbal sharing with the client of personal information, feelings about the client, self, or the counseling relationship. Self disclosures may be intentional or spontaneous.

Jourard (1964, 1968, 1971) pioneered the research and clinical examination of self-disclosure in counseling and psychotherapy as well as other forms of social interaction. He purported that people become maladjusted and eventually clients because of their lack of optimal self-disclosure to other people. Jourard (1964) was an advocate of therapist self-disclosure in counseling and therapy relationships, and he further believed that effective treatment relationships are always based upon the therapist and client's capacity for openness and self-disclosure within the context of the counseling relationship. Early studies (Forrest, 1970; Hountras and Forrest, 1970) did reveal that low-disclosing psychiatric outpatients evidenced more psychopathology than high-disclosing psychiatric outpatients, but initial level of client self-disclosure or transparency was not a predictor of brief-therapy outcome.

Truax and Carkhuff (1967) published numerous research articles and books in the 1960s and 1970s that examined therapist qualities that consistently related to favorable or poor therapeutic treatment outcomes. These authors consistently found therapist authenticity or genuineness to be the most important ingredient in effective psychotherapy relationships. Many of these studies (Truax and Carkhuff, 1967) utilized real patients in real therapy situations.

Contemporary researchers and clinicians (Bridges, 2001; Cashwell, et. al., 2003; Cooper, 1998; Curtis and Hodge, 1994; Edwards and Murdock, 1994; Farber, 2006; Forrest, 2002; Hill and Knox, 2001; Maroda, 1991) report that therapist self-disclosure occurs rather infrequently in therapy, and that counselors most frequently self-disclose about their professional backgrounds and tend not to disclose about intimate personal experiences and behavior. Disclosures between male and female therapists and therapists of different racial or ethnic backgrounds generally tend to be very similar although African American clients may have a stronger preference for counselor self-disclosure in specific areas. Self-disclosure is used by therapists and mental health workers to establish trust and understanding, model appropriate behavior for clients, normalize client feelings and experiences, teach new behaviors and copings skills, develop new or different modes of inquiry and discovery, help the client better manage powerful affects, and utilize countertransference more effectively as a tool for constructive change in the therapeutic process (Cashwell, et al., 2003; Cooper, 1998; Curtis and Hodge, 1994; Farber and Sohn, 2007; Roes, 2004).

Therapists and counselors tend not to self-disclose when the disclosure would move the focus of therapy away from the client and would burden or confuse the client, overstimulate the client, contaminate the transference, blur boundaries between client and counselor, or be overly intrusive for the client (Hill and Knox, 2001).

Therapist self-disclosure can create feelings of personal vulnerability, and it is impossible to know in advance how the therapist's disclosures will impact the therapist, client, therapeutic relationship, or therapeutic process.

Therapist classifications according to self-disclosing behavior (Dalenberg, 2000, 2004) and examinations of the relevance and importance of therapist self-disclosure in training/education programs with special clinical populations (Brown, 2004; Goodman et al., 2004; Wei and Heppner, 2005) consistently emphasize the therapeutic efficacy of this particular quality or style of therapist behavior.

Several therapist practice guidelines are presented in this chapter. Importantly, the practicing clinician needs to disclose with clients who have difficulty establishing a working therapeutic alliance and observe how clients respond to their disclosures, explore client response to disclosures, and use this feedback to implement ongoing therapeutic interventions.

Self-disclosure is an essential, but complicated pathway (Farber, Khurgin-Bott and Feldman, 2009; Kirschenbaum and Jourdan, 2005) to client growth and change. More research (Halbur and Halbur, 2006) based upon the interactions of real clients within the context of actual counseling and psychotherapy relationships needs to be completed, and researchers also need to examine areas such as the timing of disclosures, client and counselor readiness for disclosures, and specific topical impact of disclosures upon the process and outcome of the therapeutic process. Additional research (Kahn et al., 2008) needs to focus on the effects of a diversity of issues related to real client self-disclosure in psychotherapy.

Chapter 3

Therapist Theoretical-Orientation and Self-Disclosure in Psychotherapy

INTRODUCTION

As indicated in chapters 1 and 2, counselor self-disclosure is an inevitable, if not desirous and beneficial, ingredient in all counseling and psychotherapy relationships. In many situations throughout the course of the therapeutic process, self-disclosure is a highly useful and valuable therapeutic tool. It is also clear that some counselors and therapists self-disclose more frequently in their professional relationships with clients than other counselors and therapists. The content, quality, and depth or personal parameters of therapist self-disclosure also vary significantly between therapists and counselors.

There are a multiplicity of reasons and explanations for the divergent frequency, uses, content, and other variables associated with counselor self-disclosure. As several contemporary and earlier clinicians and researchers have indicated (Bugenthal, J.T.F., 1966; Edwards and Murdock, 1994; Halbur and Halbur, 2006; Hill and Knox, 2001; Jourard, 1964; Kahn et al., 2008; Peterson, 2002; Rogers and Dymond, 1954; Vogel, Wester, and Larson, 2007), the counselor or therapist's theoretical orientation seems to be a better predictor of counselor self-disclosure than many other demographic variables.

This chapter examines counselor theoretical orientation and approach to self-disclosure. Psychoanalytic and psychodynamically-oriented, humanistic and existential, client-centered or person-centered, cognitive-behavioral, family and marital, group therapy, and "mechanistic" theoretical orientations and approaches to counselor or therapist self-disclosure in psychotherapy are discussed. Multicultural issues, sexual orientation of the therapist, and various other factors can also impact both therapist theoretical orientation and approach to self-disclosure in treatment relationships.

PSYCHOANALYTICAL AND PSYCHODYNAMICALLY-ORIENTED THEORETICAL ORIENTATIONS AND APPROACH TO SELF-DISCLOSURE

Freud (1912, 2000) commented on therapist self-disclosure, saying, "the physician should be impenetrable to the patient, and be a mirror, reflecting nothing but what is shown to him" (p. 18). Traditional psychoanalysts and psychodynamically-oriented psychotherapists (Fenichel, 1945; Goldstein, 1994) view therapist self-disclosure as a strictly verboten behavior within the context of the analytical or therapeutic relationship. Analysts believed that any therapist self-disclosure would contaminate the therapeutic relationship and the analytic process. Psychoanalytic authors (Edwards and Murdock, 1994; Fenichel, 1945) have strongly opposed the use of self-disclosure in their relationships with patients. Peterson (2002) indicates that the traditional psychoanalytic authors have been most strongly "opposed to the practice of self-disclosure because they argue that disclosure could distort the client's transference and thus prevent the resolution of that transference" (p. 22). Historically, an effective resolution of the "transference neurosis" constituted a "cure" in psychoanalysis (Forrest, 2002).

Psychoanalysts and psychodynamically-oriented therapists have also viewed self-disclosure as being symptomatic of therapist countertransference. Dynamically-oriented clinicians have long viewed countertransference as a manifestation of the neurotic or unresolved conflicts of the analyst and emphasize that countertransference should ideally be eliminated from the therapeutic relationship (Fenichel, 1945; Fleiss, 1942; Forrest, 2002; Fromm-Reichmann, 1950). Contemporary analysts and psychoanalytically-oriented psychotherapists (Hahn, 2000; Slakter, 1987; Tansy and Burke, 1989) view countertransferences as an inevitable and even desirable aspect of the psychotherapeutic or analytic process. Modern analytically-oriented clinicians (Cooper, 1998; Forrest, 2002; Maroda, 1991, 1999) realize that therapist self-disclosure can be used as a tool to make unconscious conflicts, affects, and experiences conscious, help the client develop a more reality-based sense of self, and generally benefit the development and well-being of the patient.

Therapist disclosure of countertransference material is currently viewed as both clinically appropriate and therapeutic (Forrest, 2002; Maroda, 1994). Forrest (2002) generally

> advocates sharing countertransference material with clients, and guidelines for the therapeutic management of this complex and sometimes difficult therapeutic task are outlined . . . countertransference can also be used as (1) a diagnostic tool, (2) a barometer of client change or index of on-going treatment

> progress, and (3) a vehicle for enhancing counselor self-awareness and facilitating on-going counselor personal growth and education . . . in contrast to the viewpoints and interpretations of the early analysts, countertransference can be a well-spring for constructive growth and change in virtually all psychotherapy relationships. (pp. 82–83)

Finally, it should be noted that Freud both understood and acknowledged the therapeutic uses of countertransference, and he also self-disclosed dreams, personal experiences, and early childhood memories with his patients (Goldstein, 1994). Ferenczi (1950/1919), Reik (1948), and Sullivan (1953) emphasized that the analyst or counselor is a "human being." Reik (1948) states, "The psychoanalyst is a human being like any other, and not a god. There is nothing superhuman about him. In fact, he has to be human. How else could he understand other human beings? If he were cold and unfeeling, a "stuffed shirt" as some plays portray him, he would be an analytic robot or a pompous, dignified ass who would not gain entry to the secrets of the human soul" (p. 154).

It is clear that contemporary counselors and therapists with psychoanalytic and psychodynamically-oriented theoretical orientations are much more likely to utilize self-disclosure as a therapeutic tool in their relationships with clients than therapists with these theoretical orientations who practiced several decades ago. Nonetheless, analytic and dynamically-oriented counselors continue to be generally less self-disclosing in their therapeutic encounters than counselors with other theoretical orientations and backgrounds.

HUMANISTIC AND EXISTENTIAL THEORETICAL ORIENTATIONS AND APPROACH TO SELF-DISCLOSURE

Jourard (1964, 1968, 1971) was one of the first humanistic-existential psychotherapists. As indicated in chapter 2, Jourard wrote extensively about the various roles of self-disclosure in effective psychotherapy and counseling relationships as well as mental health in general. As a humanistic-existential therapist, Jourard believed that therapist and client self-disclosure or transparency is an essential ingredient in productive and effective therapeutic relationships. He also believed that healthy self-disclosure was essential to good mental health and that non-disclosing individuals become emotionally conflicted as a result of their lack of self-disclosure and authenticity.

Carl Rogers (1951) is also recognized as the father of client-centered therapy. However, Rogers (1961) also identified himself as an existential-humanistic therapist and noted,

> I have been forced to recognize that the most important ingredient in creating this climate (a therapeutic climate) is that I should be real. I have come to realize that only when I am able to be a transparently real person, and am so perceived by my client, can he discover what is real to him. The essence of therapy, as I see it carried on by myself and others, is a meeting of two persons in which the therapist is openly and freely himself and evidences this perhaps most fully when he can freely and empathically enter into the world of the other [client]. (p. 88)

Rogers (1961) further indicates "we find, for example, that in helpful relationships, it is likely that the therapist functions as a real person, interacting with his real feeling. In the less helpful relationships, we frequently find that the therapist functions as an intelligent manipulator, rather than his real self" (p 89).

Weiner (1983) also indicates that humanistic psychologists and therapists value self-disclosure as a therapeutic tool. Peterson (2002) states, "humanistic therapy emphasizes genuineness or the ability of the therapist to be freely himself or herself and to practice unconstrained honesty. This orientation also values congruence which refers to a therapist's openness regarding his or her feelings and attitudes" (p. 23). Humanistic authors believe that when the therapist is genuine, congruent, and self-disclosing, this encourages authentic disclosure from the client as well. This author also notes that humanistic therapists value the ethical principles of fidelity or "truth telling."

Finally, Goldstein (1994) summarizes the historic humanistic-existential therapist stance: "[They] regarded authenticity and genuineness in the therapeutic relationship as a necessary prerequisite for patient openness, trust, self-knowledge, the enhancement of the capacity for intimacy, and personality change" (p. 420). Hill and Knox (2001) note that therapist self-disclosure is used more often by humanistic-experiential therapists than psychoanalytic therapists. They also add that therapist self-disclosure is helpful in the immediate process of therapy.

CLIENT-CENTERED OR PERSON-CENTERED THEORETICAL ORIENTATION AND APPROACH TO SELF-DISCLOSURE

As indicated in the earlier discussions of humanistic-existential therapist viewpoints and approaches to self-disclosure in psychotherapy, Carl Rogers (1942, 1951, 1961) developed the client-centered approach to counseling and psychotherapy. Recent authors (Cepeda and Davenport, 2006; Cook, Biyanova and Coyne, 2009; Halbur and Halbur, 2006; Kirschnenbaum and Jourdan, 2005; Ponterotto, et. al., 1995; Simone et al., 1998) refer to this general model of counseling and therapy as the person-centered approach.

The person-centered approach to counseling or therapy emphasizes the importance of both therapist and client self-disclosure in therapy.

Rogers (1957) stressed the importance of therapist genuineness in the therapeutic relationship: "he is freely and deeply himself, with his experience accurately represented by his awareness of himself" (p. 97). Rogers did not encourage therapists to indulge in indiscriminant self-disclosure or expression of feeling, but he did stress that therapists must not repress or cover up their genuine feelings and responses from their clients.

Klein et al. (2002) reviewed the empirical literature examining the relationships between therapist congruence or genuineness and outcome and other therapy change processes. Of the 77 studies examined, "34% showed a positive relation to outcome; none were negative. The majority of the positive results came from research within client-centered settings" (p. 396). Importantly, Klein et al. (2002) state,

> congruence or genuineness should be recognized as a key psychotherapy treatment parameter and a potent change process . . . congruent responses may involve self-disclosure of personal information and life experiences. They may also entail articulation of thoughts and feelings, opinions, pointed questions, and feedback on client behavior. Genuine responses require mindful attention and self-reflections. Congruent responses are honest. Genuine responses are not disrespectful, overly intellectual, or insincere although they may involve irreverence. They are authentic and consistent with the therapist as a real person with likes, dislikes, beliefs, and opinions. (p. 398)

The client or person-centered approach to therapy and self-disclosure also emphasizes the importance of client self-disclosure in effective counseling and psychotherapy relationships. Truax and Carkhuff (1967) reported that as early as the second interview, level of patient self-disclosure provides a reasonably accurate prediction of therapy outcome. However, Forrest (1978, 1994) also found that self-disclosure among alcoholic patients predicted treatment outcome. Initially high self-disclosing military alcoholics more frequently entered individual and group therapy, persisted in treatment, and sustained prolonged sobriety more often than lower self-disclosing military alcoholics.

Kirschenbaum and Jourdan (2005) indicate that much of the latest psychotherapy outcome research demonstrates the presence of "common factors" in the therapeutic relationship. These "common factors" rather than particular therapeutic approaches or orientation account for therapeutic outcomes and change. These factors include therapist warmth, respect, empathy, genuineness or self-disclosure, positive relationships, and trust. However, Kirschenbaum and Jourdan (2005) also state that while, "certain amounts and types of self-disclosure by the therapist may be helpful, too much or inappropriate self-disclosure can be harmful" (p. 43). Kirschenbaum and Jourdan (2005) and Norcross (2002) emphasize that the value of empathy, unconditional positive regard, congruence, therapist genuineness or self-disclosure, management of countertransference, and repair of alliance ruptures are consistently supported by the latest generation of psychotherapy process-outcome research.

Therapists need to recognize and be more aware of their personal self-disclosing or "congruence style" and also be able to discern the needs and expectations of their clients with regard to self-disclosure, authenticity, and genuineness within the therapeutic relationship (Kirschenbaum and Jourdan, 2005; Klein et al., 2001; Vogel, Wester and Larson, 2007). Counselor or therapist self-awareness and sensitivity (Forrest, 2002) are always key ingredients in effective psychotherapy relationships.

COGNITIVE-BEHAVIORAL THEORETICAL ORIENTATION AND APPROACH TO SELF-DISCLOSURE

Albert Ellis (Patterson, 1966; Forrest, 2008) is the innovator, most widely recognized author, and advocate of cognitive-behavioral therapy in the world. He has published several hundred research and professional articles and more than eighty books over the past fifty years dealing with RET or REBT (Rational Emotive Therapy/Rational-Emotive Behavioral Therapy). The essential technique of rational-emotive therapy (Patterson, 1966)

> is active, direct teaching . . . after the initial stage, the counselor assumes an active teaching role to reeducate the client. The rational-emotive counselor thus uses logic and reason, teaching, suggestion, persuasion, confrontation, reindoctrination, indoctrination, and prescription of behaviors to show the client what his irrational philosophies are, to demonstrate how these lead to his emotionally disturbed behavior, to change his thinking . . . and thus his emotions, replacing these irrational philosophies with rational ones. (pp. 115–116)

Ellis' writings and professional training workshops (Forrest, 1994) have always been rife with personal self-disclosures. His personal self-disclosures pertaining to self-esteem, dating and courtship, and sexual behavior have long been extremely candid, humorous and entertaining, instructive, and provocative or even somewhat anxiety provoking to many of his students and trainees.

Dryden (1990) examined the specific role of self-disclosure in rational-emotive therapy (RET). Using the ABC framework of RET (Ellis, 1966), she indicates that it can be very useful for the therapist to disclose personal experiences to the client as a means of explaining the origin of psychological problems. Peterson (2002) reports that Dryden

> tells clients about how she overcame her anxiety and irrational thoughts regarding her own stuttering problem as an example of how RET can be helpful treatment. By emphasizing his or her own weakness, the therapist also demonstrates human fallibility. This demonstration of weakness by the therapist is vitally important to the RET theory that all humans are equal in their humanity and no human is more valuable than another. (p. 23)

According to Peterson (2002) and Dryden (1990), self-disclosure is a necessary ingredient for successful therapy. Peterson (2002) also notes that self-disclosure is not only ethical, but on the basis of this model, a rational-emotive therapist "who refrained from self-disclosure would be violating the ethical principle of beneficence" (p. 23). Thus, cognitive-behavioral therapists from this theoretical orientation (RET/REBT) and approach to therapy have likewise expressed their opinions pertaining to the ethics of self-disclosure in psychotherapy.

It should be noted that the behavioral therapists, social learning therapists, rational-emotive behavioral therapists (REBT), and other related "schools" or approaches to cognitive-behavioral therapy also address the uses, gains, and potential risks associated with therapist self-disclosure in psychotherapy (Forrest, 1997, 2002; Jameson, Stadter and Poulton, 2007; Roes, 2004; Vogel, Wester and Larson, 2007).

Glasser's reality therapy (1965, 2000) and choice theory approaches to therapy (1998, 2001, 2003, 2005) are also essentially cognitive-behavioral therapies. Reality therapy and choice theory therapists (Wubbolding, 2009) utilize here-and-now, cognitive, behavioral, action-oriented treatment interventions. Helping clients behave more responsibly and rationally have always been core ingredients in the reality theory approach (Glasser, 1965). Glasser (2000, 2003, 2007) has always been very self-disclosing in his writings, lectures, and clinical demonstrations. Reality Therapy in Action (2000) actually includes Dr. Glasser's verbal dialogues, thoughts, feelings, and self-disclosures as he conducts therapy with persons who are experiencing various emotional and relational difficulties. Choice theory (Wubbolding, 2009) also helps clients make better life choices and relies upon therapist and client self-disclosures.

Brief relational therapy (BRT) has been utilized as a cognitive-behavioral and psychodynamic treatment model for patients with personality disorder diagnoses. Safran and Muran (2005) indicate that a key feature of BRT is making "intensive use of therapist self-disclosure and collaborative exploration of what is taking place in the therapeutic relationship" (p. 14). Brief solution-focused therapy and DBT (dialectical behavioral therapy) are also cognitive-behaviorally based therapies that actively utilize self-disclosures.

FAMILY AND MARITAL THERAPY THEORETICAL ORIENTATIONS AND APPROACH TO SELF-DISCLOSURE

The early contributors to the field of family therapy (Ackerman, 1954; Bateson et al., 1956; Haley, 1959, 1963; Minuchin, 1965; Satir, 1967; Whitaker, 1958) emphasized that family and marital systems are units or systems with their own relatively unique set of interactive dynamics. The family system is subject to a form of homeostatic balance, which can only be understood and potentially modified vis-à-vis the interactive behaviors, roles, and communication within the system. This approach or orientation shifted the aim of therapy from individual change within the therapy relationship to family change. Individual change was believed to be a by-product of familial or marital relationship change. Correspondingly, the style and therapeutic approach of family and marital therapists changed from passive noninvolvement to active involvement.

Haley (1959, 1963) discusses "therapeutic interventions" that therapists utilize in both marriage and family therapy. These interventions may involve defining rules, modifying pathological styles of communication, paradoxical interventions, and imposing paradoxical situations emphasizing the positive and undermining the couples' or family's typical ways of labeling the relationship. Minuchin (1965) describes the role of the therapist in conflict-resolution family therapy as "somewhat like the director of a play, asking family members to try to comply with his instructions, pressuring them to seek other than their usual repertoire or interaction, demanding that they fulfill his expectations" (p. 303).

Bowen (1978) has also written extensively about the therapist's various roles in family and marital therapy. In accord with the writing and work of other family and marital therapists, Bowen (1978) does not discuss the specific concepts of therapist or patient self-disclosure. However, he does disclose personal anecdotes about his own family of origin conflicts and relational difficulties.

The treatment of alcoholic marital relationships has been examined by Paolino and McCrady (1977). According to these authors, the essential goal of marital therapy is "to help the couple increase the over-all rewardingness of their relationship, to assume that positive consequences will result from desired behaviors, and that these positive consequences will not occur when undesired behavior, such as drinking occur" (p. 161). Paolino and McCrady (1977) explore various couples treatment-oriented techniques and methods. However, they do not address the specific issue of self-disclosure in couples therapy.

Forrest (1991, 1994) indicates that therapists who work with alcoholic families and couples didactically teach family members and marital couples about relationships and roles, role slippage and reversals, and role behaviors. He also notes (Forrest, 1991) that it is important for therapists to help families and couples openly explore feelings, cognitions and beliefs, and relational/transactional realities that are associated with dysfunctional patters of role slippage and role reversal. While failing to discuss the specific issue of therapist and client self-disclosure in family and couples therapy, Forrest (1991, 1994, 2001) and other clinicians (Black, 1982; Wegscscheider 1981) emphasize that alcoholic and chemically-dependent family systems and couples maintain communication styles or patterns of interacting that do not involve open, honest, and consistent self-disclosures. Recently (Farber and Sohn, 2007) clinicians have addressed several nefarious issues related to self-disclosure within the explicit contexts of marriage and marital therapy.

GROUP THERAPY THEORETICAL ORIENTATION AND APPROACH TO SELF-DISCLOSURE

Psychoanalytically-oriented group therapists have historically (Slavon, 1956; Wolf, 1950) maintained a traditional psychoanalytic nondisclosing role in group therapy work. Analysts have viewed the group leader or therapist as a father figure while viewing the group as a complimentary mother figure or extension of the family. The primary role function of the group analyst (Wolf, 1950) is to "guide his patients to full awareness of social integration" (p. 80). Wolf (1950) also indicates that group analysis (1) demonstrates to each patient that he shares his problems with others, (2) acts as a buffer against despair, and (3) provides social rewards such as general acceptance and a sense of belonging. The group spontaneously fosters an "endless" source of provocation and passionate interconnection that is steeped in self-disclosure. This process furnishes material for "analysis and good will."

More contemporary psychoanalytically-oriented group therapists (Fuhriman and Burlingame, 1994; Ruitenbeck, 1969; Yalom, 1995) generally continue to avoid self-disclosing behavior in group treatment.

The person-centered (Kirschenbaum and Jourdan, 2005), cognitive-behavioral (Forrest, 1991, 1994), gestalt (Pearls, 1969), encounter group, psychodrama or T-group (Yalom, 1995), support group and self-help (alcoholics anonymous, narcotics anonymous, al-anon, etc.) group orientations and approaches of the past three decades (Bratter and Forrest, 1985; Ogborne and Glaser, 1985; Forrest, 2009) have generally encouraged group therapist openness and self-disclosure. The evolution of virtually all theoretical orientations and approaches to group therapy over the past forty years has included the trend toward more therapist self-disclosure and openness in group treatment settings.

Yalom (1995) has perhaps examined the various facets of contemporary group therapy more extensively than any other psychiatrist or behavioral scientist in the world. His contributions to the theory and practice of group therapy also include a rather extensive examination of several aspects of self-disclosure in group psychotherapy. According to Yalom (1995), the "primary sweeping objection to therapist transparency is based on the traditional analytic belief that the paramount curative factor is the resolution of patient-therapist transference" (p 101). He indicates that the group therapist "sets a model of interpersonal honesty and spontaneity," and also notes "total disinhibition and unrestrained expression of all feelings is no more salubrious in therapy groups than in other forms of human encounter . . . the therapist must set a model which includes honesty as well as judicious restraint . . . interacting as a group member requires, among other things, that the therapist accept and admit his fallibility" (p 92).

Successfully treated patients (Yalom, 1995) "have usually expressed a wish that the therapist had been less aloof, more involved in the group. Yet none of the patients wanted the therapist to have contributed more of their personal lives or problems to the group" (p 103). Burlingame et al. (2001) propose specific group leader techniques for facilitating member self-disclosure as well as indicating that leader self-disclosure "should be measured, matched to the stage of the group's development, and focused on real-time observations that have relevance for the group" (p 376). Forrest (1994) has also noted that therapist and patient self-disclosure in group therapy is very much a part of the process of initiating healthy change and learning upon the part of the group members.

MECHANISTIC THEORETICAL ORIENTATIONS AND APPROACH TO SELF-DISCLOSURE

Mechanistic approaches to therapy and behavioral change can be viewed as treatment models that primarily involve the therapist doing something to the patient. These approaches or theoretical orientations to therapy generally involve doing something therapeutic *to* the client or patient rather than doing something therapeutic *with* the patient. Mechanistic treatment models and interventions are essentially less relationship-oriented approaches to behavioral change and personality growth. Therapist self-disclosure is extremely limited, or for most clinical purposes, does not occur in the context of mechanistic therapies.

Hypnosis, biofeedback training, EMDR (Hartung and Galvin, 2003; Schaad, 2009), and biological psychiatry are mechanistic models of behavioral change. While patient self-disclosure of symptoms is essential to all of these treatment approaches, therapist self-disclosure is not an essential clinical component of these treatment approaches. For example, the hypnotist or biofeedback clinician tells the patient to relax, induces a trance, or "hooks" the patient up to a machine and teaches him or her how to reduce blood pressure, pulse rate, and so forth. Very few contemporary psychiatrists (Glasser, 2003, 2005; Fleming, 2008) actually practice "talk therapy" or relationship psychotherapy with their patients. Psychiatrists prescribe medications to their patients, tell them when and how much of the medication to take, and attempt to assess the impact of the medication on the patients' depression or mental illness. Psychiatrists generally see their "patients" for ten to fifteen minutes each two to three months, and the therapeutic relationship is viewed as secondary or tertiary component to the change process. Medication is the "real" or primary agent of change according to the biological psychiatry approach.

Eye movement desensitization and reprocessing (EMDR) (Hartung and Galvin, 2003; Schaad, 2009) and other mechanistically-oriented therapies also may be used effectively within the context of the relationship-oriented therapies. Interestingly, Schaad (2009) and Shapiro (2001) note that in actual practice, EMDR may perhaps best be described as a client-oriented, interactive, interactional, intrapsychic, cognitive, and behavioral body-oriented therapy. The key elements of all these modalities are integrated to treat the client as a whole person.

Hartung and Galvin (2003) note that while EMDR and "energy-based" treatments for addicts have been described in the clinical literature, the long-term benefits of these protocols have not been substantiated. However, Schaad (2005, 2009) has indicated that client openness and self-disclosure is key to the effectiveness of these therapeutic interventions while self-disclosure is generally minimal or avoided by clinicians who utilize these treatments.

SUMMARY

Therapist and client self-disclosure is essential to the process of effective psychotherapy and counseling. All therapists rely upon their clients to disclose personal thoughts, feelings, behaviors, and other sources of conflict in order to better assess, understand, utilize, and implement appropriate treatment interventions and simply help clients change (Vogel, Wester and Larson, 2007). In effect, counselors and therapists may be unable to help or at least are limited in their efforts to therapeutically help noncommunicative and non self-disclosing clients. However, the role and importance of therapist self-disclosure in general as well as self-disclosure by therapists from the same or different theoretical orientations are more complex and less agreed upon components of the therapeutic process.

Therapist self-disclosing behavior exists on a continuum and may vary according to the therapist's professional training (Jameson, Stadter and Poulton, 2007), theoretical orientation, and treatment approach. Psychoanalysts and psychodynamically-oriented psychotherapists generally tend to be very non self-disclosing. The humanistic, existential, and client-centered or person-centered therapists tend to be very open, authentic, and self-disclosing or transparent in their therapeutic relationships (Halbur and Halbur, 2006). Cognitive-behavioral therapists are generally in the middle of the continuum of therapist self-disclosing behavior. However, this author has observed that Albert Ellis and William Glasser (2000, 2007) have been very self-disclosing in their clinical training and demonstrations as well as in their publications.

Therapist self-disclosure within the context of family and marital therapy, group therapy, relational therapy, and more "mechanistic" treatment models was also discussed in this chapter. Mechanistic approaches to therapy or mechanistic treatment interventions include hypnosis, biofeedback, psychotropic medications, EMDR, relaxation training, and assertion training. Group therapists are also generally self-disclosing in their therapeutic work. Mechanistic treatment interventions tend not to involve therapist self-disclosures. However, it should be noted that when mechanistic treatment modalities are utilized by a therapist *within* the context of an ongoing psychotherapeutic relationship or process, the therapist may be quite disclosing within the context of the overall therapeutic process (Schaad, 2005, 2009).

Chemical dependency counselors (Forrest, 2002, 2006, 2008; Roes, 2004) are often quite self-disclosing in their counseling relationships with clients, and recovering chemical dependency counselors may be especially prone to disclosing personal recovery anecdotes and experiences with their clients.

Finally, it is important to note that therapists from any school or theoretical model of counseling and psychotherapy may vary considerably with regard to personal self-disclosure style. Ultimately, the "nuts and bolts" of therapist self-disclosure in psychotherapy—whether to disclose or not, when to disclose, and what and how to disclose personal material—is effected by a multiplicity of complex therapist, client, and relational dynamics. Nonetheless, therapist and client self-disclosures are core ingredients in all effective psychotherapy relationships independent of the therapist's theoretical orientation to therapy (Forrest, 2008; Halbur and Halbur, 2006; Myers and Hayes, 2006; Vogel, Wester and Larson, 2007).

Chapter 4

The Effects of Therapist and Client Self-Disclosure in Psychotherapy

INTRODUCTION

As discussed in chapters 2 and 3, therapist or counselor self-disclosure occurs within the context of virtually all psychotherapeutic relationships. While individual therapists and clinicians from different models or "schools" of therapy and counseling may differ significantly in their uses and approaches to self-disclosure in therapy, most agree that the therapist-patient self-disclosure nexus is a complicated but essential ingredient in the psychotherapy process.

The issue of patient or client self-disclosure in therapy appears to be less complicated and less controversial. Simply put, it is difficult, if not at some point impossible, to do effective psychotherapeutic work with non-disclosing persons. The psychotherapist depends upon the patient to openly and honestly disclose his or her experiences, thoughts, and emotions within the context of the therapeutic relationship. This allows the therapist to assess the patient's actual treatment needs and establish appropriate treatment and interventions.

The effects of therapist self-disclosure on the therapeutic relationship have been investigated with some degree of consistency and depth for over four decades (Farber, 2006; Goodheart, C.D., Kazdin, A.E., and Sternberg, R.J., 2006; Jameson, P., Stadter, M. and Poulton, J., 2007). The results and findings from these studies are reviewed in this chapter. To the contrary, the effects of patient self-disclosure (Kahn et al., 2008) on therapists and the therapeutic relationship have rarely been investigated or discussed in the psychotherapy research and clinical practice literature. However, the results and general implications from this realm of self-disclosure research are discussed in this chapter. The clinical impact of client self-disclosure in psychotherapy is also examined in this chapter. Case illustrations pertaining to the effects of therapist and patient or client self-disclosure in psychotherapy are also included in this chapter.

THE EFFECTS OF THERAPIST SELF-DISCLOSURE IN PSYCHOTHERAPY

Most of the existing research (Hill and Knox, 2001; Kasper, Hill and Kivlighan, Jr., 2008; Kirschenbaum and Jourdan, 2005) pertaining to therapist self-disclosure in psychotherapy involves analogue designs, which are actually simulations of therapeutic interactions rather than actual therapeutic interactions between a therapist and client. These analogue studies of therapist self-disclosure in individual therapy often involve undergraduate or graduate psychology students and research designs that employ audiotapes, written transcripts, or videotapes of hypothetical therapy sessions. Hill and Knox (2001) reviewed eighteen analogue studies of therapist self-disclosure in individual therapy and found that "14 reported positive perceptions of therapist self-disclosure, 3 reported negative perceptions, and 1 reported mixed findings" (p. 413).

Watkins (1990) also reviewed analogue findings related to therapist self-disclosure. Hill and Knox (2001) conclude from this study that "therapists who self-disclosed in a moderate or non-intimate way have been viewed more favorably and have elicited more client self-disclosure than therapists who did not disclose at all, who disclosed a lot, or who disclosed very intimate material" (p. 413). These authors also indicate that "non-clients typically perceive therapist self-disclosure positively" (p 413).

Hill et al. (1988) examined three studies, which included two data sets that evaluated the immediate outcome of therapist self-disclosures on clients. These investigations involving actual therapists and clients reported positive effects. Commenting on the findings from these studies, Hill and Knox (2001) state, "clients gave the highest ratings of helpfulness and had the highest subsequent experiencing levels (i.e., involvement with their feelings) to therapist self-disclosures. Interestingly, therapists gave the lowest ratings of helpfulness to self-disclosures, perhaps because disclosure made them feel vulnerable" (p 414). A further analysis of this data (Hill, Mahalik, and Thompson, 1989) revealed that "reassuring disclosures were viewed as more helpful than challenging disclosures in terms of both client and therapist helpfulness ratings and subsequent client experiencing levels" (p 414).

These general findings once again demonstrate how variable and inconsistent therapist and client perceptions of therapist self-disclosures can be pertaining to the impact and efficacy of therapy.

Knox et al. (1997) conducted a qualitative analysis of client perceptions of the effects of helpful therapist self-disclosure in actual long-term therapy and found that therapist self-disclosure fostered client insight and also made the therapist seem more real and human. Hill and Knox (2001) note that these factors improve therapeutic relationships and help clients feel more normalized as well as reassured. Furthermore, therapist self-disclosures also helped clients feel better, served as a model for positive change, and reinforced client self-disclosure and honesty in therapy.

Hill and Knox (2001) reviewed nine studies of the effects of therapist self-disclosure on distal or ultimate therapeutic outcome. Their findings were mixed. According to Hill and Knox (2001),

> of studies using a correlational method, no relationship was found between the frequency of therapist self-disclosures and client, therapist, or observer judgments of treatment outcome in six studies, a negative relationship was found between frequency of therapist self-disclosure and therapists' ratings of client improvement in another study, and two other studies using other methodologies found positive effects of therapist self-disclosure on treatment outcome. Another study (Barrett and Berman, 2001) found that clients who received more reciprocal therapist disclosures (i.e. self-disclosure in response to similar client self-disclosures) liked their therapists more and had less symptom distress after treatment, although they did not increase in the number or intimacy of their own self-disclosures. (p. 415)

Summarizing their review of the effects of therapist self-disclosures, Hill and Knox (2001) state:

> the analogue literature suggests that non-clients generally have positive perceptions of therapist self-disclosure . . . the literature about actual therapy indicates that humanistic-experiential therapists disclose more than psychoanalytic therapists, therapists disclosed infrequently in therapy, therapists disclosed mostly about professional background and rarely about sexual practices and beliefs, therapists had many reasons for disclosing as well as several indications of when they would avoid disclosing, and disclosures were perceived as helpful rather than unhelpful in terms of the immediate outcome of therapy, but the effects on the ultimate outcome on therapy remain unclear. (p. 415)

One study (Wells, 1994) involving eight adult clients reported that therapist self-disclosure resulted in generally negative results. It is interesting to note that three of the eight clients indicated that their trust and confidence in their therapist was low at the time of the disclosure. Peterson (2002) also reviewed this study and indicated "(1) all eight participants reported some degree of disappointment, disillusionment, or surprise . . . however, six of the participants described a range of positive and negative emotions following the disclosure, and (2) four of the participants reported that the disclosure helped them perceive their therapist as involved, trusting, and understanding" (p. 29). Thus, half of the clients in this investigation did report some positive effects associated with therapist self-disclosure.

Simi and Mahalik (1997) reported that 60 percent of clients indicate that their therapists have self-disclosed personal information, experiences, or feelings during therapy sessions. While the literature on therapist self-disclosure indicates that this therapist tool or technique is usually appropriate, helpful, and therapeutic, some clients may respond differently to therapist disclosures and, for example, possibly feel anxious, frightened, or threatened by the intimacy and closeness that can be fostered by therapist self-disclosure (Peterson, 2002).

Therapist self-disclosure can also be used to demystify the counseling process. Litrell (1998) indicates that research supports the sharing of "two or three" self-disclosures in an opening counseling session as optimal. According to Litrell (1998), clients found this technique reassuring and realize that they are being helped by a real person.

Bridges (2001) identifies several clinical sources of gain associated with therapist self-disclosure. These include opening up space for "deep therapeutic" engagement between the therapist and patient, and enhancing self-perception, affective experiences, and the relational connection. Bridges (2001) states "intentional self-disclosure is a valuable tool in a therapeutic relationship that facilitates exploration, introduces new perspectives on self in relationship, and conveys to the patient the possibility of creating a new, healing object relationship . . . therapist self-disclosure may be a helpful vehicle to make conscious unconscious affect or relational dynamics that influence the treatment and benefit the patient's development" (p. 22). She also notes that the therapist's intentional self-disclosures can lead to unexpected "growth-fostering clinical opportunities."

A recent review (Kirschenbaum and Jourdan, 2005) of hundreds of journal articles, books, and book chapters on the effects of the client-centered or person-centered therapy approach clearly demonstrates that (1) when therapists consistently provide high levels of the "core conditions" of effective psychotherapy (nonpossessive warmth, empathy, and genuineness) within the context of the therapeutic relationship, and (2) when the client perceives these essential therapist qualities at least to a minimal degree within the therapeutic encounter, then (3) clients generally evidence constructive personality change and growth. Gurman (1977), Norcross (2002), Truax and Carkhuff (1967), and Truax and Mitchell (1971) also provide compelling research evidence from numerous studies involving thousands of clients and patients over the past forty-five years and essentially reach the same conclusions: therapists and counselors who are accurately empathetic, nonpossessively warm, and genuine or self-disclosing are effective. Kirschenbaum and Jourdan (2005) indicate "much of the latest research on psychotherapy outcome has demonstrated that, rather than particular approaches, it is certain 'common factors' in the therapy relationship" that account for therapeutic change. These authors also add that "certain amounts and types of self-disclosure by the therapist may be helpful, too much or inappropriate self-disclosure may be harmful" (pp. 43–44).

Finally, one of the more consistent research findings in the area of the effects of therapist self-disclosure in therapy is that self-disclosing therapists and counselors are seen as more attractive by their clients (Cashwell, et. al., 2003; Goodyear and Shumate, 1996). This is particularly true when therapist disclosure statements are positive in nature. Therapists may also tend to self-disclose more to clients manifesting greater psychopathology (Kelly and Rodriguez, 2007).

The theoretical literature pertaining to cultural diversity and counselor self-disclosure generally reports positive results as a result of counselor self-disclosure (Sue and Sue, 1999). However, Cherbosque (1987) found that Mexican clients rated nondisclosing counselors as both more attractive and "expert" and also tended to perceive self-disclosing counselors as behaving unprofessionally. American and Caucasian respondents (Cashewell et al. 2003) indicate a preference for counselor disclosure about interpersonal relationships and success/failure. Thus, the research evidence suggests that counselor self-disclosure as a multicultural counseling or therapy strategy produces mixed results. These studies also rely heavily upon analogue research designs.

In summary, the value of therapist self-disclosure or genuineness as one of the central ingredients in effective individual psychotherapy is rather strongly and consistently supported by the historic as well as latest generation of psychotherapy process-outcome research literature (Gurman, 1977; Kirschenbaum and Jourdan, 2005; Lambert, 1992).

THE EFFECTS OF PATIENT OR CLIENT SELF-DISCLOSURE IN PSYCHOTHERAPY

As noted in chapter 2, patient self-disclosure in therapy (Kahn and Vogel, 2008) has rarely been a topic of investigation in the psychotherapy process-outcome literature. The clinically-oriented psychotherapy process-outcome literature also rarely addresses the specific relationships between patient self-disclosure in therapy and therapeutic efficacy or the interactive dynamics between the patient and therapist. Simply put, the effects of patient or client self-disclosure in psychotherapy and counseling have not been extensively studied.

As discussed in chapters 2 and 3, an early investigation by Truax and Carkhuff (1967) found that as early as the second interview patient self-disclosure level provided a reasonably adequate prediction of final therapy outcome. Patients who were more self-disclosing and open very early in psychotherapy demonstrated better therapeutic outcomes than patients who were more guarded and nondisclosing during initial therapy sessions. Patient self-disclosure was assessed from the actual audio and video tapes of real therapy sessions in this study (Truax and Carkhuff, 1967).

It was also noted in chapter 2 that earlier studies (Forrest, 1970, 1978, 1994; Hountras and Forrest, 1970) reported relationships between levels of patient self-disclosure and general psychopathology, and levels of patient self-disclosure and sobriety as well as treatment outcomes. Forrest (1970) found that initial level of client transparency or self-disclosure did not predict brief therapy outcome. This study involved psychiatric outpatients who completed six individual therapy sessions that were conducted by doctoral level counseling psychology students. Patient self-disclosure levels (low, medium, and high) were based upon SDQ scores (Self-Disclosure Questionnaire, Jourard, 1964).

Another investigation using the SDQ (Forrest, 1978, 1994) to assess initial levels of patient self-disclosure found this measure (SDQ) was related to treatment outcome. Alcoholic patients in this study who were initially higher self-disclosers (1) tended to more often actively engage in individual therapy, group psychotherapy, Alcoholics Anonymous (AA), and other treatment modalities deemed appropriate by treatment staff, and (2) more often established and sustained sobriety then did alcoholic patients who were initially significantly lower self-disclosers on the SDQ. All patients in this study were active duty (army) military personnel. It should be noted that the author (Forrest, 1994) reported that some of the low-disclosing patients in this study actually deteriorated during the six-month treatment interval. Forrest (1978, 1994) also suggested that "perhaps a minimal level of patient self-disclosure must be present before the patient is ready or able" to actively enter any rehabilitation program.

Patient self-disclosure has also been related to adjustment and severity of psychopathology. As touched upon briefly in chapters 2 and 3, Forrest (1970) and Hountras and Forrest (1970) found that low-disclosing psychiatric outpatients evidenced significantly greater psychopathology on the MMPI clinical scales than did high-disclosing psychiatric outpatients. These investigations (Forrest, 1970; Hountras and Forrest, 1970) also suggested that extremely low and extremely high self-disclosing psychiatric outpatients manifested more severe psychological symptoms on the MMPI than did moderately self-disclosing psychiatric outpatients.

Interestingly, Forrest (1978, 1994) also noted in his investigation of self-disclosure and sobriety that low-disclosing alcoholics manifested a total disclosure score that was very similar to the low-disclosing group total disclosure score in the psychiatric outpatient study (Forrest, 1970). All of these investigations utilized the Self-Disclosure Questionnaire (SDQ) (Jourard, 1964; Jourard and Lasakow, 1958) to assess patient levels of self-disclosure. Denial and other defense mechanisms specific to alcoholism and the personality structure of chronic problem drinkers and concordant severe psychopathology may cause and reinforce addictive behavior as well as impede movement in the direction of seeking help. Patient self-disclosure (Forrest, 1994, 2005) may also be related to all of these processes.

It should be emphasized that the effects of client or therapist self-disclosure in psychotherapy are determined and impacted by a multiplicity of factors. For example, Jourard (1964, 1968) and Jourard and Lasakow (1958) found that women disclose more than men, Caucasians disclose more than African Americans, people generally disclose more to their mothers than their fathers, high self-disclosure is associated with positive feelings toward parents, while low self-disclosure is associated with attitudes of dislike toward parents, applicants for clinical services at a university counseling center were lower disclosers than matched groups of students who had not sought psychological services, areas or topics of self-disclosure vary among different groups of people, older people disclose less as they age, and religious affiliation impacts patterns of self-disclosure. Thus, a diversity of cultural, social, familial and interpersonal as well as intrapersonal factors affect patterns of self-disclosing behavior (Farber and Sohn, 2007).

These realities associated with self-disclosure in psychotherapy have numerous potential implications for therapists, patients, and the mental health professions. For example, therapeutic outcomes may be more favorable when patients and therapists share more common patterns or styles of self-disclosure. Perhaps matching therapists and clients according to self-disclosure patterns might facilitate more optimal treatment outcomes? Potential patient and therapist biases associated with race, gender, ethnicity, sexual orientation, or other barriers to constructive treatment relationships might be identified and minimized via the self-disclosure rubric.

EFFECTS OF PATIENT OR CLIENT SELF-DISCLOSURE ON THERAPISTS AND THE THERAPEUTIC RELATIONSHIP

The psychotherapy and counseling research-oriented literature generally and consistently indicates the importance of patient or client openness and self-disclosure as an important ingredient in the development of a psychotherapeutic relationship or therapeutic alliance (Farber, 2006; Farber, Khurgin-Bott and Feldman, 2009; Kirschenbaum and Jourdan, 2005; Norcross, 2002). However, this body of literature has not explored the various clinical effects of patient self-disclosure on therapist adjustment and behaviors, the patient-therapist process or relational dynamics, or treatment outcome and efficacy.

To the contrary, a good deal of the historic (Fenichel, 1945; Fromm-Reichman, 1950; Reik, 1948) as well as contemporary analytic and psychoanalytically-oriented clinical literature (Kernberg, 1975, 1994) does address the impact of patient self-disclosure, behavior, beliefs, and effect upon the psychotherapist, treatment relationship, and even therapeutic outcome. As noted in earlier chapters, a few highly recognized contemporary therapists from other "schools" of counseling and psychotherapy (Ellis, 1996, 2004; Glasser, 2000, 2003; Halbur and Halbur, 2006; Lejuez and Hopko et al., 2005) also openly discuss their personal therapeutic responses and reactions to patient self-disclosures. Actual therapy vignettes and case studies are utilized by some of these authors to demonstrate the clinical impact of patient self-disclosure on the therapist, therapeutic process, and treatment outcome.

Patient or client self-disclosures to the therapist can provide a broad spectrum of cognitive/intellectual, emotional, behavioral or transactional, and social-interpersonal responses in the therapist (Forrest, 2002; Kahn et al., 2008). For example, clients who disclose to their therapists that they are actively considering suicide or physically harming another person generally stir feelings of great concern, anxiety, or possibly fear in the therapist. These disclosures also trigger a number of therapist thoughts and behaviors such as discussing treatment alternatives involving hospitalization, developing a non-suicide/non-self-other harm contract, the real need for more intensive care, possible notification of family or others, initiating a duty to warn action, referral for immediate medication assessment, consultation with a colleague or psychiatrist, and so forth.

The disclosure by a patient or client of sexual feelings or physical attraction to the clinician (Bonitz, 2008; Gabbard, 1996) can likewise precipitate a diversity of therapist responses. Most counselors are able to quickly and directly process this type of client self-disclosure in the therapeutic context and move on with the ongoing work of therapy, but such disclosures may also result in premature treatment termination, a time-limited therapeutic stalemate and resolution phase, client referral to another therapist, or on rare occasions, be the catalyst for an inappropriate and iatrogenic sexual relationship between the counselor and the patient. Clearly, different therapists and counselors tend to utilize generally similar and appropriate therapeutic interventions in response to sexualized patient self-disclosures pertaining to the counselor, but this arena remains conflictual and inherently thorny for all clinicians.

The self-disclosures of substance abusing (Forrest, 1995, 1999, 2002, 2009) patients as well as antisocial, impulsive, and character-behavior disordered persons are often steeped in distortions and lies. Chemically dependent persons (Forrest, 2001, 2009) routinely lie to their therapist and other people in their lives about virtually anything or everything not simply their addiction or addiction-focused behaviors. It can be extremely difficult for counselors and therapists who work with this patient population to simply discern if and when the patient is telling the truth or presenting information accurately within the context of the therapeutic relationship. These factors limit the therapist's ability to intervene effectively and/or help many clients. The basic matter of client capacity for honesty in therapy impacts all therapeutic relationships in numerous ways. Therapists and patients or clients can become sickened by self-disclosures that are dishonest, distorted, and deceptive. Patients actually make themselves progressively more ill and conflicted vis-à-vis their lies and dishonesty with the therapist and others, and therapists or counselors can actually be harmed by the process of repetitively being lied to by a patient or over the course of spending years of being lied to by perhaps thousands of patients. Honest patient self-disclosures are essential to the process of healthy growth and change in therapy as well as life!

The following case illustrations are presented to demonstrate the impact and some of the effects of therapist and patient self-disclosure in psychotherapy.

Case One: Mrs. C. was a sixty-three-year-old married woman who initially scheduled a consultation session with the author to discuss her concerns about her daughter and grandchildren. The patient indicated that her daughter and son-in-law were "meth addicts," and she had grave concerns for their children. Mrs. C. also reported that she had been a meth addict since the "late sixties" and that she had also been "addicted to every drug on the face of the earth" for over forty years. Her first husband reportedly "made" her work as a street prostitute for a number of years, her second husband had just been released from prison after spending twenty years being incarcerated for homicide, and her current husband (sixth), who was described as being a very successful businessman, was reportedly drinking a pint of "JD" every night.

Mrs. C. did indicate that she had been "clean and sober" for nearly four years during the late 1980s.

During the initial session, Mrs. C. quickly shifted into her recent (one to two years) history of "pathetic medical care," briefly discussed several physicians who had been treating her for "pain" and other various medical conditions with opiod, benzodiazapine, and psychotropic medications. She asked if the author would help her find "a good attorney" to "sue the fuckin' bastards." She reported that she had acquired considerable wealth over the years and despite her "brain damage from all the drugs," she was going to "make them see what they've done to me." The patient indicated that she had completed eleven long-term (twenty-eight days or longer) residential chemical dependency treatment programs and had been "active in AA and NA on and off" over the past four decades.

At the end of the initial consultation, Mrs. C. stated that she had not actually been in contact with her daughter and grandchildren in several months. She also "thought" that her daughter and son-in-law were not presently involved with "meth," but they had "gotten a restraining order" against her six months earlier. Mrs. C. seemed extremely angry, confused, and reported that she had been "drinking on and off, maybe a pint a night," but concluded her session by saying that she might reschedule for another session, noting "I've had a lot of bad experiences with shrinks."

The self-disclosures of this client during her initial consultation with the author were intense, related to many facets of her life, and somewhat overwhelming. It was almost impossible to simply slow down or deter the patient's level of disclosures and, indeed, this initial session was one of the most personally impacting experiences I have had in the course of some thirty-five years of practicing psychotherapy. I felt "flooded" by the patient's continual self-disclosing behavior in the course of a fifty minute therapy session! Her self-disclosures were steeped in abuse, chronic and dehabilitating polydrug dependence, manipulation, seriously disturbed interpersonal and familial relationships, criminal behavior, pathological sexual behaviors, anger, domestic violence and chronically conflicted treatment, self-help, and psychotherapy experiences. She did not reschedule for a second consultation session or therapy.

Case Two: John W. was referred to the author by a residential chemical dependency treatment center following a very brief (five day) hospitalization. The patient and the treatment staff felt that he did not need to complete a twenty-eight-day inpatient program, but follow-up psychotherapy had been recommended by the program staff. The patient explained to the author during the second therapy session that he had been released from a federal prison a month earlier and was "working off" his prison sentence with the

DEA and FBI by "setting up" large drug deals (cocaine) across the United States. He also showed the author $300,000 in cash that he had in the trunk of his car. Over the course of two or three months of weekly individual therapy, the patient disclosed various aspects of the drug deals that he was involved with via the DEA and federal government. He also disclosed that he had previously completed an MBA from a major Midwestern university, owned a number of businesses, and he had been addicted to cocaine for over fifteen years. He abruptly terminated therapy after three months of treatment by calling the therapist form a federal prison in Florida, indicating that he had been "re-arrested."

This patient's self-disclosures to the author were initially met with some level of near disbelief, but it readily became apparent that he was being open and honest in therapy. My awareness of the frequency of drug busts, amount of cocaine routinely involved in these arrests (ten to fifteen kilos of cocaine), and the amount of money involved provoked some anxiety and even personal fear. Nonetheless, my focus with the patient remained on his recovery and the risk factors associated with his decision to "work it off" with the federal government.

Case Three: Mary Ann was a twenty-four-year-old woman who was referred to the author for a psychological evaluation by her attorney following her third arrest for driving under the influence of alcohol (DUI/DWAI). The patient was an attractive, bright, and articulate woman who initially reported she was not exactly sure why her attorney had referred her for evaluation, but verbalized that "maybe my evaluation will help my attorney get me off the charge." During the initial course of taking the patient's family, social, and medical histories, she became increasingly anxious and defensive and eventually told the author "this is too damned personal . . . my personal life is my business, and nobody else's . . . no offense to you, Doctor, but I'm not doing it . . . that damned judge can do whatever he wants with me." The client terminated the evaluation process at that point.

The patient's decision to terminate the evaluation process and her prior disclosure to the author that she believed that the evaluation might get her "off" a legal charge were surprising. It was also very unusual to simply have a patient terminate an evaluation that, was originated by an attorney. However, it also become readily apparent to the author that Mary Ann felt very uncomfortable and apprehensive about self-disclosing anything about herself and her clinical history.

These case illustrations clearly demonstrate that patient self-disclosure significantly impacts both the therapist and the therapeutic relationship. Patient self-disclosures are also self-impacting. The client in case three may have clearly sensed that the clinician's role was not to "get her off" the DUI charge and the assessment process may have even precipitated her increased awareness that her self-disclosures could be personally damaging to her legal case!

Patient self-disclosures are always essential to the initiation and maintenance of the psychotherapeutic process. However, patient or client self-disclosures may also impact the therapeutic process at any juncture. A lack of patient self-disclosure early in treatment may jeopardize the future of the therapeutic relationship or impede treatment progress and the establishment of a productive and working therapeutic alliance (Forrest, 1997). Too much or prematurely intense patient self-disclosures can threaten or adversely impact the therapist, therapeutic relationship, and/or patient. Premature treatment termination and therapist anxiety and insecurity may be triggered by patient over-self-disclosing behaviors early in treatment and at other junctures in the therapeutic process.

In truth, patient or client self-disclosure, like therapist self-disclosure, can always be "for better or worse" in psychotherapy. Patient self-disclosures can enhance the therapeutic relationship and are always essential to the therapist's understanding of the patient as well as the therapist's utilization of efficacious therapeutic interventions. The patient also potentially grows and changes via the medium of his or her therapeutic disclosures within the context of the treatment relationship. Therapists and the therapeutic relationship often grown and adaptively change as a result of the patient's disclosures. Yet, patient self-disclosures can always be potentially self-damaging and destructively impact both the therapist and the therapeutic alliance.

SUMMARY

Therapist self-disclosures are generally viewed as favorable by clients and result in more client self-disclosures in therapy (Farber, 2006; Hill et al., 1988; Hill and Knox, 2001; Watkins, 1990). Therapy self-disclosure studies involve analogue designs as well as actual patients. Therapist self-disclosures have also been shown to foster client insight, help patients feel better, improve therapeutic relationships, and reinforce patient self-disclosures and honesty in therapy. (Hill, et. al., 1997; Hill and Knox, 2001; Roes, 2004) However, other studies report that therapist self-disclosure in therapy (Peterson, 2002; Roes, 2004; Wells, 1994) can result in negative and/or mixed effects on patients.

Kirschenbaum and Jourdan (2005) recently reviewed hundreds of journal articles, books, and book chapters on the effects of person-centered or client-centered therapy and concluded that "common factors" in therapy account for therapeutic change. These factors include therapist genuineness and/or self-disclosure. However, these authors also indicate that certain amounts and types of therapist self-disclosure may be "too much," inappropriate, or even harmful.

Patient self-disclosures (Kahn et al., 2008; Forrest, 2009) also impact the process and outcome of psychotherapy. Patients or clients who are more open and self-disclosing very early in psychotherapy (Truax and Carkhuff, 1967) have better therapeutic outcomes than nondisclosing patients. Low-disclosing psychiatric patients also exhibit more severe psychopathology than high-disclosing psychiatric patients (Forrest, 1970; Hountras and Forrest, 1970). However, Forrest (1970) found that initial level of patient self-disclosure did not predict brief therapy outcome.

Forrest (1978, 1994) also reported that high-disclosing alcoholic patients more often become actively engaged in individual and group therapy as well as Alcoholics Anonymous, and they also were more successful in their efforts to establish and sustain sobriety than low-disclosing alcoholic patients.

The psychotherapy and counseling literature has long emphasized the general clinical importance of patient or client openness and self-disclosure as a precursor to the development of the working and productive therapeutic alliance and constructive therapeutic relationships. (Farber, 2006; Forrest, 1997; Forrest, 2008; Myers and Hayes, 2006; Norcross, 2002) However, this body of literature has not examined the various effects of patient self-disclosure (Farber, Khurgin-Bott and Feldman, 2009) on therapist adjustment and behaviors, the patient-therapist process or relational dynamics, and treatment efficacy.

This chapter examines a number of potential therapist responses to different types of patient or client self-disclosures. The various forms and content of patient self-disclosures (Kahn et al., 2008) may impact different therapists in myriad ways. The impact of patients' lies and distortions on therapists is discussed at some length in this chapter, and three case illustrations are also presented to demonstrate the impact and effects of patient and therapist self-disclosure in therapy.

It is very apparent that patient and therapist self-disclosures are essential to all forms and models of effective psychotherapy. However, therapist as well as patient self-disclosures in psychotherapy can always result in any number of unpredictable positive of negative therapeutic effects. The therapist's or patient's self-disclosures can in effect be for better or worse at any juncture in the psychotherapeutic process, and the self-disclosing behaviors of either party can impact the self, other, and therapeutic relationship in a diversity of ways.

Therapist and client self-disclosure is always a core ingredient in effective psychotherapeutic relationships. And yet paradoxically, patient or client self-disclosures as well as therapist self-disclosures always have the potential to sicken the self, other, or therapeutic alliance as well as other human relationships. For these reasons, therapists and counselors need to remain especially sensitive, aware, focused, and restrained in their use of personal self-disclosures in psychotherapy. Many experienced and seasoned therapists understand all too well the potentially damaging nature of long-term exposure to upsetting and toxic patient self-disclosures. Therapists also need to be vigilant in their efforts to exude healthy and therapeutically efficacious self-disclosures in therapy rather than exposing their patients and clients to potentially damaging or psychonoxious self-disclosures (Forrest, 2002, 2009) in their treatment relationships.

Chapter 5

Ethics and Therapist Self-Disclosure in Psychotherapy

INTRODUCTION

A multiplicity of ethical guidelines and principles pertaining to virtually every facet of the practice of psychotherapy have been developed over the past fifty years. These ethical guidelines and principles have been utilized by all of the behavioral science professions that are involved in the education and training of therapists and counselors. The ethical standards that have been developed within the professions of clinical and counseling psychology, social work, counselor education, family and marriage counseling, addictions counseling, mental health counseling, and psychiatry share a number of core principles and precepts. These general ethical standards have not historically been applied to the specific realm of therapist self-disclosure in counseling and psychotherapy relationships. Nonetheless, several basic professional ethical standards and precepts can be more generally applied to the arena of therapist self-disclosure in therapy.

Ethical guidelines and standards are usually not rigid or black-and-white in nature. Indeed, the ethical standards of conduct pertaining to any profession can be subject to diverse and often conflicting viewpoints and interpretations (Kitchner, 1986).

As indicated throughout this text, the general viewpoints on self-disclosure in psychotherapy are diverse. Likewise, perspectives on the ethics of therapist self-disclosure in psychotherapy differ significantly between therapists and different "schools" of psychotherapy. This chapter will address ethical guidelines for therapist self-disclosure in psychotherapy and chemical-dependency counseling. Therapists need to be aware of the ethical as well as clinical ramifications of self-disclosing interventions in therapy. This chapter will also elucidate the complexity of ethical issues associated with therapist self-disclosure in psychotherapy. The therapist's ongoing clinical decisions and choices about self-disclosing in therapy relationships always have numerous ethical ramifications.

ETHICS AND THERAPIST SELF-DISCLOSURE

A small number of publications address the specific ethics of therapist self-disclosure in psychotherapy. These articles also tend to be brief, theoretical, and very general in nature. Peterson (2002) states, "The ethicality of a particular (therapist) self-disclosure is likely to depend on the content of the disclosure, the therapist's rationale for the disclosure, the personality traits of the client to whom the disclosure is made, and the specific circumstances surrounding the disclosure" (p. 21).

Peterson (2002) also indicates that the American Psychological Association's "Ethical Principles of Psychologists and Code of Conduct" provides a number of principles and guidelines that pertain to the matter of therapist self-disclosure in psychotherapy. According to Peterson (2002),

> Ethical Standard 1.19 (1992) is one of the APA guidelines most closely related to the controversy surrounding self-disclosure. This guideline states, "Psychologists do not exploit persons over whom they have supervisory, evaluative, or other authority such as . . . clients or patients" (p. 1602). APA Ethical Principle E contains a similar statement that highlights the fact that psychologists have power over their clients and must therefore avoid using that power in an exploitative manner. Although these ethical principles do not refer specifically to the issue of self-disclosure, concerns about client exploitation often are raised in relation to therapist self-disclosure. (p. 22)

Koocher and Keith-Spiegel (1998) and Saccuzzo and Johnson (2007) have recommended that psychologists utilize both the APA ethical standards as well as several other core ethical principles in their professional relationships and activities. The ethical standards recommended by these authors include nonmaleficence (not harming patients), beneficence (maintaining the goal of helping others), being just, being faithful, and respecting autonomy. According to Peterson (2002) nonmaleficence and beneficence

> are the two ethical principles that are most often addressed in relation to self-disclosure because these principles are implicit in many writings about the clinical usefulness of therapist self-disclosure. If in a given situation, self-disclosure is a highly useful therapeutic tool, then disclosing to clients may be ethical

> according to the principle of beneficence. However, if therapist self-disclosure impedes the therapeutic process, practicing disclosure may violate the principle of nonmaleficence. (p 22)

Self-disclosure needs to be self-monitored and continually regulated by therapists as they interact with their patients. Self-awareness, self-scrutiny, and healthy self-regulation are essential therapist precursors to the optimal use of self-disclosures in psychotherapy. Bridges (2001) notes that the "fiduciary principle must be honored and informs therapists' decisions regarding disclosure" (p. 22). She (Bridges, 2001) addresses the ethical-clinical continuum of issues related to therapist self-disclosure in psychotherapy by pointing out that

> [t]herapists guard against excessive disclosures, disclosures that shift the focus away from the patient, or disclosures that might harm monitoring the effect of such interventions on the patient and the treatment process . . . therapists employing intentional self-disclosures are advised to remain patient focused, rely upon the patient's resources and expertise, model emotional honesty, and share their view of the clinical situation at hand . . . exploration of the multiple interpersonal and intrapsychic meanings of the disclosure to the patient and the treatment process is essential. (pp. 22–23)

Related to the ethical-clinical continuum of issues associated with self-disclosure in therapy, Peterson (2002) states, "the question that must be addressed is not whether it is ethical to self-disclose to clients but rather what content, for what reasons, to whom, and under what circumstances should an ethical therapist disclose?" (p. 22).

Peterson (2002) also addresses each of these questions pertaining to the ethics of therapist self-disclosure in therapy. It should be noted that the clinical and theoretical viewpoints and opinions that are presented in each of these areas are diverse and often very contradictory in nature.

The content of therapist self-disclosures can be viewed as one ethical measure. Several authors (Bridges, 2001; Peterson, 2002; Roes, 2004; Ruth, 2007; Wells, 1994) indicate that it is ethically appropriate for the therapist to disclose personal information pertaining to education, training, experience, general theoretical-orientation, and expected duration of treatment or treatment goals. In fact, it may be unethical to fail to provide patients with these forms or content of self-disclosures.

The content and disclosure of information or material pertaining to the personal life and experiences of the therapist constitutes another form of self-disclosure, which encompasses a diversity of ethical issues. Wachtel (1993) indicates that the therapist's self-disclosures pertaining to experience outside of the therapy relationship can be inappropriate or unethical, whereas therapist disclosures about feelings and experiences related to the client and the therapeutic relationship are beneficial and ethical. Clinicians (Epstein, 1994) have warned against therapist self-disclosure of personal problems, and inappropriate therapist disclosures may even be related to sexual involvement with patients or suicidal behavior by patients. However, Epstien (1994) also notes that it would be unethical for the therapist to fail to disclose any personal information that would affect the patient's ability to make treatment decisions.

A number of authors (Peterson, 2002; Wells, 1994) have developed categories of therapist self-disclosing behavior and suggested that some categories are more ethical than others. For example, Wells (1994) views the therapist's admission of therapeutic mistakes or errors in the therapeutic relationships as a category of therapist self-disclosure.

The ethical parameters pertaining to the content of therapist self-disclosures may be confusing and can involve many antithetical viewpoints. For example, Knox et. al (1997) reported that therapists disclosures involving "personal nonimmediate information" about past personal difficulties, family, and social/leisure activities benefited their clients in all cases. Clearly, the clients in this study (Peterson, 2002) viewed "therapist self-disclosures about personal experiences as an ethical and beneficial technique" (p. 24).

The ethical principle of autonomy (APA Ethical Standard 4.02, 1992) emphasizes that "therapists should foster independence and self-reliance and that they should respect the rights of individuals to decide how to live their lives," and Ethical Principle D indicates "psychologists are aware of cultural, individual, and role differences, including those due to age, gender, race, ethnicity, national origin, religion, sexual orientation, disability, language and socioeconomic status" (Peterson, 2002, pp. 23–24).

These factors have led some therapists (Hawkins and Bullock, 1995; Koocher and Keith-Spiegal, 1998; Kooden, 1991; Perlman, 1991; Mahalik, et al, 2000) to conclude that disclosing one's sexual orientation or religion is an ethical imperative. Some homosexual therapists report that there are many benefits to disclosing the therapist's sexual orientation to gay clients, but these authors also noted that self-disclosing one's sexual orientation is potentially unethical and exploitative (Perlman, 1991).

The reasons for therapist self-disclosures are many and varied. However, the therapist's motivation and reasons for self-disclosing are also important factors in the ethical assessment of this aspect of therapist behavior. Several authors conclude (Brown and Walker, 1990; Farber, 2006; Goldstein, 1994; Gutheil and Gabbard, 1995; Roes, 2004) that it is exploitative and, thus, unethical for therapists to self-disclose for the reason or purpose of meeting personal needs. Therapist disclosure of personal problems can also be unethical or damaging to the patient. Goldstein (1997) noted that therapist self-disclosures should be used for empathetic rather than selfish reasons.

Ethical reasons for therapist self-disclosure (Curtis and Hodge, 1994) include facilitating empathy and trust, modeling behavior, normalizing the patient's feelings and struggles, and helping patients express feelings and emotions.

As Peterson (2002) notes, the client's perception of the therapist's reasons for self-disclosing is a very important ethical consideration. However, the client's perception and beliefs about the therapist's reasons for self-disclosing can be influenced by myriad factors and, thus, it is always very difficult for therapists to predict how client's will respond to their self-disclosures. This is why it is always important for therapists to use foresight and reasoned decision making when they self-disclose to their clients.

A number of authors (Epstein, 1994; Farber, Khurgin-Bott and Feldman, 2009; Forrest, 2002; Goldstein, 1994; Peterson, 2002) have suggested that certain patient populations may be more likely to be helped or harmed by therapist self-disclosures. The ethical principles of nonmaleficence and beneficence can also be applied to the matter of which patients will probably be most helped or most harmed by therapist self-disclosures. This is another factor that makes it important for therapists to give forethought to the decision to self-disclose to patients.

Goldstein (1994) suggested that patients with boundary difficulties, reality conflicts, dependency issues, intimacy difficulties with the therapist, repressed strong emotions, and those who are very self-absorbed might be clinical subgroups for whom therapist self-disclosure could violate the ethical principle of nonmaleficence.

Clinicians (Greenberg, 1990) have also suggested therapist self-disclosures may be clinically or ethically inappropriate in therapeutic relationships with children, adolescents, and elderly patients. However, it has also been argued that therapist self-disclosure can be both therapeutic and ethical in treatment relationships with these clinical populations (Paponchis, 1990).

Goldstein (1997) revealed that one of her patients had been harmed by her personal lack of self-disclosure about a severe physical illness. Vamos (1993) also disclosed that her clients were emotionally harmed by her decision to not disclose that she was suffering from bereavement. As noted earlier in this chapter and elsewhere (Brown, 2004; Counselman, 1997; Dalenberg, 2004; Muller, 2009), several clinicians who work with clinical populations involving trauma, feminist issues, and gender-related conflicts suggest that therapist self-disclosures can be both ethical and therapeutic in the treatment relationship.

Bram (1995) discusses the ethical parameters of therapist self-disclosure associated with illness and even impending death and encourages therapists in these situations to practice fidelity vis-à-vis self disclosure regarding the details of their illness or medical condition. The therapist's disclosures about these personal matters can help the client make more informed decisions about continuing therapy with the therapist and other matters. However, Bram (1995) also notes that the therapist's disclosure of illness can adversely impact the client. Therapist self-disclosure of health problems can potentially inhibit patient self-expression, foster anxiety in the client, or possible be exploitive if the therapist seeks attention or empathy via these transactions. The therapeutic alliance can be affected and the treatment relationship terminated as a result of therapist disclosure of illness or impending death.

APA Ethical Standard 4.08 (1992) pertains to therapist disclosures in these difficult situations. Peterson (2002) indicates that this ethical standard

> dictates that psychologists must make an effort to anticipate and plan for any interruption of services due to the psychologist's illness or death . . . as well, standard 4.09 states that psychologists not abandon their clients. These standards suggest that when a therapist's illness will interfere with treatment or may result in death, the therapist is obliged to prepare the clients for these possibilities and to help them find treatment elsewhere . . . under these circumstances, (therapist) self-disclosure seems to be virtually an ethical imperative. (pp. 28–29)

APA Ethical Standard 1.13 (1992) also states that

> psychologists recognize that their personal problems and conflicts may interfere with their effectiveness. Accordingly, they refrain from undertaking an activity when they know or should know that their personal problems are likely to lead to harm to a patient, client . . . or other person to whom they may owe a professional or scientific obligation. In addition, psychologists have an obligation to be alert to signs of, and to obtain assistance for, their personal problems at an early stage in order to prevent significant impaired performance. (p. 1601)

It has also been argued that therapists have a right to personal privacy and, thus, may not be required to disclose matters pertaining to personal illness, health, or loss (Goldstein, 1997). Perhaps the most important ethical obligation the therapist has in these matters is to make every effort to minimize potential harm to the patient.

In view of the diverse and generally unpredictable effects or results of therapist self-disclosure on patients and the therapeutic relationship, it is always incumbent upon therapists to be aware of and employ their professional ethical guidelines when self-disclosing in psychotherapy. Therapists also need to think through their personal ethical beliefs pertaining to self-disclosure in various clinical situations prior to self-disclosing to patients.

ETHICS AND THERAPIST SELF-DISCLOSURE IN CHEMICAL DEPENDENCY COUNSELING

The professional ethics of chemical dependency counselors (Dove, 1995) "follows logically from the ethics which apply to health care in general, medicine, and mental health" (p. 21). The chemical dependency treatment field has established ethical standards of practice at the regional, state, and national levels over the past few decades. Insurance fraud, breech of confidentiality, self-referral practices, misrepresentation of treatment "success rates," "free initial evaluations," dual relationships, reimbursement policies, and "kickbacks" for referrals (Dove, 1995) are but a few of the thorny areas of ethical misconduct that have historically plagued the chemical dependency treatment field.

Dove (1995) notes that "some of the unethical behaviors which have led to the present status [of the chemical dependency treatment field] could have been prevented with an appropriate training program in applied professional ethics" (p. 19). He indicates that the goals for a continuing education program in applied professional ethics for chemical dependency counselors should include the following: "(1) increase counselor (staff) sensitivity to ethical issues which arise in day-to-day practice, (2) improve the ability of counselors (staff) to reason about ethical dilemmas, (3) counselors (staff) should be able to formulate a plan of action based on the ethical analysis and follow through with the plan, and (4) counselors (staff) thereby improve coping mechanisms for tolerating the ambiguity of ethical decision making" (p. 28).

Forrest (2002) indicates that countertransference issues impact every facet of ethical practice in the chemical dependency and mental health treatment fields. He stresses that therapist-client sexual involvements can always be related to the problem of countertransference. This form of ethical violation is invariably harmful to patients, the therapeutic relationships, and ultimately therapists as well. Forrest (2002) also points out that ethics generally refers to the science of moral values and duties or the study of the ideal human character, actions, and behavior. Ethical conduct involves conforming to professional standards of conduct and behavior. According to Forrest (2002), countertransference is "at the heart of the dynamic processes that underlie sexual contact between chemical dependency counselors and clients and virtually every other form of unethical counselor behavior" (p.88). This author goes on to briefly discuss therapist characteristics that may be related to unethical behaviors and faulty ethical decision making.

The recent chemical dependency counselor and treatment literature (Roes, 2004) often tends to address the therapeutic and possible clinical effects of therapist self-disclosure rather than specifically addressing the ethics of therapist self-disclosure in this relatively specific treatment arena. However, Roes (2004) wisely provides ethically sound guidance pertaining to "The Rules of Self-Disclosure." For example, Rule Five directs that counselors "self-disclose in response to legitimate questions about your licensure, certification, education or experience" (p. 27). Within the context of Rule Four, Roes (2004) states "your clients have a right to know your qualifications and theoretical orientation. Appropriate self-disclosure can help clients become more comfortable that you are qualified and able to understand their problems" (p. 27). Although the specific issues of ethics and ethical guidelines for counselor self-disclosure are never discussed by Roes (2004), his rules of self-disclosure, warnings on the dangers of self-disclosure and praises of self-disclosure include ethically appropriate and wise guidance.

Roes' (2004) clinical summary pertaining to the uses of self-disclosure by addictions professionals is also in concert with the ethical parameters of therapist self-disclosing behavior that have been addressed in this chapter and throughout the book. In this regard, Roes (2004) generally recommends

> you should only choose to self-disclose when the disclosure is thoughtfully designed to accomplish a specific therapeutic goal. If you strictly limit the amount you disclose, then it is possible to self-disclose to normalize client behavior, build rapport, encourage client disclosure, or support other therapeutic goals. This is only possible when you avoid self-disclosures that may damage client self-esteem, blur boundaries, shift focus in an unhelpful way, or meet your needs instead of the client's. (p. 28)

It is apparent that the emergent chemical dependency counseling and treatment field has also become increasingly aware of the various ethical issues associated with therapist or counselor self-disclosure. All behavioral health subspecialty groups have become more aware of the importance of establishing and maintaining ethical practice standards over the past decade or two. Continuing education and ongoing training programs; professional ethical monitoring and regulation agencies at various levels of local, state, and federal government; and individual practitioner sensitivity to ethical practice standards and guidelines have all been central to this process. The recent proliferation of lawsuits against physicians, psychologists, mental health workers, social workers, hospitals, educators, and all human service and behavioral health providers has dictated the development of more clearly defined and regulated professional ethical practice guidelines and standards within each specific subspecialty arena. However, there continues to be a diversity of viewpoints and opinions about both the clinically appropriate as well as ethically appropriate parameters of therapist self-disclosure in psychotherapy (Farber, Khurgin-Bott and Feldman, 2009; Kotter, 1990; Littrell, 1998; Solomon et al., 2001).

Divergent opinions and viewpoints also surround a multiplicity of other therapist behaviors and practices. Indeed, it becomes increasingly apparent that there are relatively few areas of black or white or absolutes in the broad arena involving ethical standards of psychotherapy practice. Rather, the ethical guidelines and standards pertaining to the practice of counseling and psychotherapy are often unclear, difficult to objectify, and more simply put, steeped in grey rather than being black or white.

SUMMARY

There is no specific or definitive definition of what it means to be an ethical therapist or psychologist. However, unethical behavior can simply be defined as a breach in the minimal standards of a professional's behavior. For example, psychologists are required to follow the "code of conduct" guidelines of the Ethical Principles of Psychologists, which delineates eighty-nine such standards. A violation of this professional code of conduct constitutes "unethical behavior."

Ethics can generally be defined as "thinking about reasons in terms of values" (Behnke, 2005). Core ethical principles and values for psychologists and therapists generally include beneficence and nonmaleficence, fidelity and responsibility, integrity, justice, and respect for people's rights and dignity. Accoding to Behnke (2005), the values in these five ethical principles "play a fundamental role in setting the ethical parameters of our (psychology) profession" (p. 114).

Ethics also generally refers to the science of moral values and duties or the study of the "ideal" human character, actions, and behavior. Thus, most therapists and psychologists strive to exceed the minimal ethical standards of conduct that have been established by their professional organizations.

This chapter addresses the specific realm of professional ethics related to therapist self-disclosure in psychotherapy. A very limited number of publications address this important topic. However, Peterson (2002) has written rather extensively about the ethics of therapist self-disclosure in psychotherapy and generally reports that the content of therapist disclosures, rationale for disclosing, circumstances surrounding disclosures, and characteristics of the patient are key factors that determine the ethicality of this form of therapist behavior. Several ethical standards of the APA (1992) "Ethical

Principles of Psychologists and Code of Conduct" that pertain to therapist self-disclosure in psychotherapy were examined in the chapter. This section of the chapter was based largely upon the earlier work of Peterson (2002) and others (Goldstein, 1994, 1997; Gutheil and Gabbard, 1995).

As Peterson (2002) notes, "the literature on self-disclosure suggests that the sharing of information is often ethically appropriate and, in some cases, even ethically necessary" (p. 30). She also notes that therapist self-disclosing behavior in therapy is a very complex ethical issue. Peterson summarizes the ethics-focused literature on therapist self-disclosure in therapy by recommending that therapists consider the following questions prior to disclosing personal information to patients: "(a) Is this information necessary to protect the client's informed consent? (b) Is my purpose in disclosing this information to benefit the client or to benefit myself? (c) Will this particular client use this information in a way that is helpful? and (d) Will disclosing this information interfere with our therapeutic progress, such as by contaminating the client's therapeutic transference?" (p. 30).

Therapists clearly need to examine their personal beliefs, attitudes, motives, and feelings about self-disclosing to patients prior to engaging in this form of behavior. Counselors and therapists also need to consciously consider the various ethical vicissitudes of self-disclosure prior to disclosing personal information to patients.

A number of the ethical dilemmas pertaining to chemical dependency counselors and the chemical dependency treatment field were also addressed in this chapter. As an emergent profession, chemical dependency counselors (Dove, 1995; Forrest, 2002, 2009; Roes, 2004) are increasingly aware of the various ethical standards that guide their work. However, many chemical dependency counselors and especially recovering counselors may overutilize personal self-disclosure as a therapeutic tool (Forrest, 1994, 1997, 2002, 2008). This chapter will be especially useful for the training and professional development of many addictions counselors and chemical dependency counselors.

Finally, the ethical uses of therapist self-disclosure in psychotherapy can contribute to more efficacious therapy outcomes and potentially enhance both patient and therapist growth. As pointed out in this chapter, clinicians manifest a diversity of opinions and often conflicting viewpoints pertaining to the ethical issues of therapist self-disclosure in psychotherapy. Therapists also need to be encouraged (Behnke, 2005; Lane, 2006; Ruth, 2007) to aspire to maintain an ethical level of practice that transcends the basic rules and standards of their professions.

Chapter 6

Self-Disclosure, Addiction, and the Recovery Process

INTRODUCTION

Self-disclosure or transparency has long been a topic of relevance and interest to many professionals involved in the profession of counseling and psychotherapy. The professional psychotherapy and counseling literature pertaining to therapist and patient self-disclosure encompasses nearly six decades (Bridges, 2001; Farber, Khurgin-Bott and Feldman, 2009; Forrest, 1994, 1997, 2002; Hill and Knox, 2001; Kirschenbaum and Jourdan, 2005; Jourard, 1964, 1968; Roes, 2004; Rogers, 1951, 1961; Teasdale and Hill, 2006; Truax and Carkhuff, 1967). As noted earlier in this book, the current as well as historic self-disclosure literature has focused upon a diversity of issues. The impact of therapist self-disclosure on patients and treatment outcome, patient self-disclosure and treatment outcome, ethnic and racial background and patterns of disclosing behavior, adjustment and self-disclosure, and the ethics of therapist self-disclosure are but a few of the areas that have been examined in this text as well as the general research and clinical self-disclosure literature.

As therapists, we seem to have generally shared the basic belief that self-disclosure is a core ingredient in effective psychotherapy relationships with a diversity of patient populations. This seems to be particularly true with regard to patient self-disclosing behavior. Patient self-disclosure has been perceived as a basic prerequisite to virtually all therapeutic relationships. As noted throughout the text, therapist self-disclosure is a far more controversial issue. The various sources of debate and controversy surrounding the issue of therapist self-disclosure in general psychotherapy practice were also elucidated in earlier chapters of the book.

The various roles and dynamics of self-disclosing behaviors in the etiology of addictive disorders are examined in this chapter as well as the impact of self-disclosure on the recovery process. This chapter also explores the specific realms of therapist and patient self-disclosure in psychotherapy relationships with addicted and substance abusing patients. Alcoholics Anonymous (AA) and other self-help recovery (Cocaine Anonymous/CA, Gamblers Anonymous/GA, Narcotics Anonymous/NC, Over-Eaters Anonymous/OA) programs and models also rely upon self-disclosure as a recovery tool. Self-disclosure in the self-help literature, recovery community, and recovery process is discussed and explored in this chapter. Self-disclosure and recovery from psychological problems and major psychiatric illness is also briefly examined in this chapter. This discussion will further clarify the relevance and importance of self-disclosure in all behavioral health areas.

SELF-DISCLOSURE AND THE ADDICTIONS

The addictions and substance use disorders (Bratter and Forrest, 1985; Forrest, 1994, 1997, 1999, 2002, 2009; Shaffer, 2006) always develop as a result of multiple factors. Thus, genetic factors clearly impact the risk level or general probability for developing alcoholism or a severe drinking disorder among specific persons, the general public, or particular sub-population groups. Cultural, age, gender, race, socioeconomic, psychological-interpersonal, educational, vocational, religious-spiritual, and other variables also impact the risk individuals and groups manifest for developing alcoholism, other substance use disorders, or any form of addictive disorder. In effect, all addictive disorders are multivariantly determined and maintained (Forrest, 1997, 2002, 2009).

An inability to consistently self-disclose in a healthy and optimal manner is one key psychological-interpersonal factor in the etiology of addictive disorders. This premise is based upon the author's nearly thirty-five years of clinical experience involving the assessment and psychotherapy of thousands of alcoholics, substance abusers, addicts, and their families. Indeed, one of the earliest (Forrest, 1975) clinical observations the author reported [on] pertaining to alcoholics and problem drinkers was simply an "almost total lack of self-disclosure upon the part of these individuals." This patient population also appeared to be significantly uncomfortable and anxious in the most casual of interpersonal relations. When initially sober and/or drug abstinent, these individuals were clearly nondisclosing in their relationships with others, and most avoided or resisted self-disclosing within the context of intensive individual psychotherapy as well. At first, I attributed the guarded, defensive, and nondisclosing style of alcoholics and drug-dependant persons in the early stages of sobriety to be essentially a function of the "drying out" process or detoxification. However, several months after completing the detoxification process and with sustained alcohol and/or drug abstinence, many of these patients continued to behave in a withdrawn, apprehensive, defensive, anxious, guarded, and nondisclosing manner. Their interpersonal encounters and interactions in therapy were also consistently nondisclosing.

A few months after I began my life-long professional career in chemical dependency treatment and addictions psychotherapy, I began to interact and have significant experience with recovering alcoholics and addicts. My personal experiences in psychotherapy and the AA or recovery community began in an Army Alcohol and Drug Rehabilitation program during the Vietnam War. At this time, as I continued my clinical work with this group of persons, I continually rediscovered that most actively recovering persons are very open and self-disclosing. And it has always been my general observation that with increasing recovery time and active involvement in psychotherapy, AA or other self-help recovery programs, and sponsorship, self-disclosing behavior increases, and these persons become generally more healthy, more open and disclosing, and better adjusted.

My recovering patients who have sustained five, ten, twenty, or nearly thirty-five years of uninterrupted alcohol/drug abstinence are some of the most open and self-disclosing people I have ever known. Therapy groups, education and recovery support groups, and "open" or "closed" self-help meetings that include a number of persons with many years of sustained recovery can be rather profound human encounters that are steeped in openness, authenticity, and reciprocal self-disclosure.

As I have continued my clinical work with several thousand substance abusers and addicted patients, I have also found that the patients who were unable to make the transition from very little self-disclosing behavior to a style of more openness and disclosure were often prone to relapse or unable to sustain treatment and self-help involvement as well as abstinence and the recovery process. Many years ago (Forrest, 1975) I reported, "I have yet to see a patient maintain his or her sobriety for over six or seven months in the absence of a marked increase in self-disclosing behaviors . . . specifically, I am suggesting that long-term sobriety is contingent, in part, upon learning and engaging in an interpersonal mode which is highly self-disclosing in nature" (p. 236).

At the time, I also addressed the difficulties associated with assessing patient self-disclosure changes within the therapeutic and recovery process, but noted that I was simply attempting to convey that self-disclosure is an essential ingredient in sobriety and the recovery process. The following recent case vignette illustrates how patient self-disclosure can be related to treatment, recovery, and relapse.

Case 1: A few months ago, Bob S., a forty-year-old business owner was seen in consultation and brief therapy at the request of his family physician. He had been drinking two to three pints of whiskey a day for nearly three years and taking opiod medication for severe back pain. The patient was also scheduled to have a six-hour spinal surgery in a few weeks, and in concert with his physician, expressed very real concerns about his drinking and the surgical risks he might experience. He agreed to a brief hospitalization to be "detoxed," underwent a successful spinal surgery a few weeks later, and subsequently was seen within the context of a few individual therapy and support group sessions for the following two months. He also attended Alcoholics Anonymous one or two times a week at that juncture. The client was able to be somewhat open in individual therapy but "did not care to participate" in the support groups and on several occasions related to the group that he felt his personal life and problems were "nobody's business." He avoided any disclosures pertaining to himself in the group, openly acknowledged resenting the "personal nature of AA," soon dropped out of treatment, and resumed drinking. A couple of months later he called to say that he was leaving to enter a long-term inpatient treatment program in another state.

Addicts and substance abusers are unable or find it very difficult to self-disclose early in therapy and recovery. They have long repressed, denied, and avoided (Forrest, 1999, 2008) the many painful and traumatic realities associated within their lives. They are unable to express their feelings and emotions in a healthy manner, and they have learned and been told in myriad ways not to disclose their inner thoughts, emotions, beliefs, and experiences. They have learned to portray a mask of sanity in their interactions with others, and it should not be surprising that these individuals are chronically anxious and avoid self-disclosure in their interactions with therapists and significant others.

Drug-dependent persons are particularly non-disclosing about their drug use and dependence early in the psychotherapy process. They avoid, minimize, and distort therapeutic conversations about their addictions and drug dependence. Many also repetitively and adroitly lie to therapists and counselors about every facet of their drug use at this juncture in the therapeutic process. These patients also lie about their substance use to significant others, and they also have an uncanny ability to deny and avoid dealing with many painful realities associated with their addictions. Their limited self-disclosures while still using and early in therapy are often used in the service of the addiction process—to further justify, cover up, mask, and deny to self and others the various realities of their continual drug dependence, alcoholism, eating disorder, sexual addiction, or compulsive gambling.

Paradoxically, many of these patients are not capable of self-disclosing at this point unless they are intoxicated or under the influence of a psychoactive substance, which only serves to invalidate the reality and meaningful nature of their disclosures. Alcohol and drug-facilitated self-disclosures are always neurotic and ultimately ineffective attempts to self-disclosure in a more realistic, healthy, and therapeutic manner. Drug and addiction facilitated self-disclosures are simply not real.

The alcoholism treatment literature (Forrest, 1975, 1994, 2006, 2009) is rife with discussions of how bartenders have long been viewed as quasi-therapists by drinkers as well as the general public. Bartenders listen to many of their intoxicated patrons as they disclose or "unload" their problems, marital difficulties, and openly discuss their health, family, work, and financial difficulties. From a relational and self-disclosure perspective, this form of dialogue takes on some of the essential characteristics of a psychotherapy or helping relationship. These self-disclosing transactions may be somewhat confessional and cathartic in nature for both or all participants, and these exchanges may result in some degree of therapeutic relief for the participants. However, these quasi-therapeutic self-disclosure based interactions remain essentially neurotic. The alcoholic continues to drink alcoholically or abusively, and the core factors essential to his or her addiction and other sources of conflict remain unresolved.

This general situation is a *sine qua non* of all neurotic behavior. These self-disclosures are alcohol based and thus only prove partially beneficial. Therefore, they are fated to occur and reoccur with the same dysfunctional effect. From this perspective the addiction process can be viewed as a maladaptive repetition compulsion. I would argue that if such self-disclosing interactions were to occur on an ongoing basis for several months or a few years, in the absence of alcohol or drug intoxication, significant growth and change would be a rather natural by-product of the process. This is exactly why therapists do not consistently or routinely attempt to do individual therapy or group therapy with patients who are drunk or under the influence of other psychoactive substances at the time of treatment!

Self-disclosure is a form of communication and behavior that addicted people find difficult or are unable to engage in. The following brief case vignettes provide clinical examples of the pathological self-disclosing styles of a compulsive overeater and a gambling addict.

Case 2: Judy S. was a forty-four-year-old married mother of three children who was seen in weekly individual therapy by the author for one year. She also attended Weight Watchers and Overeaters Anonymous (OA) on a weekly basis during the year that she was actively engaged in therapy. The patient described herself as a "closet eater." Early in therapy she began to disclose that she also hid food, ate copious amounts of food in her car, and refused to discuss her eating behaviors and "weight problem" with family members or others. She also had a long history of lying to her husband, children, and extended family members about all these issues. She repeatedly told her therapist "my weight is nobody's damned business."

After a few months of therapy and self-help treatment, Judy became more open and disclosing with her therapist and family. She was also beginning to be an open and more disclosing member of OA and Weight Watchers. As she slowly began to lose weight, she was also able to be more open and self-disclosing about the trauma and profound narcissistic injury she had experienced in childhood and adolescence as well as the painful experiences and feeling of ridicule and shame associated with her adult obesity. The patient lost one hundred pounds in thirteen months and reportedly continued her self-help treatment involvement. Not only was she a different person physically, her self-esteem, social behaviors, effect, confidence, and self-disclosing style were also radically improved.

Case 3: The extended family of Bill C. scheduled an appointment with the author in hopes of initiating an "intervention" in order to get help for his gambling addiction. After spending an hour with Bill's parents and wife, a family therapy session was scheduled, and the author simply suggested that his wife invite Bill to participate in that session. Bill agreed to come to this next session, and the family and extended family was seen together a few days later. The focus of this following family session centered on the specifics of Bill's compulsive gambling and the devastating consequences of his behavior on his wife and children, in-laws and family, and himself. He had been gambling compulsively for over six years and had lost a five hundred thousand dollar home, two professional jobs, and had declared bankruptcy a year earlier. The patient was separated from his wife and children, his father-in-law was providing financial support for Bill's family, and Bill had actually started to steal money from his in-laws. Needless to say, he was no longer trusted by his wife or family, and he was generally perceived as a liar and manipulator. Bill was depressed and dependent, anxious, shamed, and guilty, but he had continued to gamble away his paycheck and whatever other monies he could get. He had also actively contemplated suicide.

Bill then began weekly individual therapy with the author; his wife and children were referred to another therapist, and she and her parents began to attend open GA (Gamblers Anonymous) meetings and Alcoholics Anonymous (AA). Bill began to attend three GA meetings a week as well as AA, and he also obtained a sponsor a few weeks later.

The patient was initially resistant to being involved in therapy but he was very attached to his wife and children, and he also openly acknowledged that he had been unable to stop gambling on his own in spite of the catastrophic financial losses he had suffered. He was initially more self-disclosing and open in therapy about his lying, manipulation, and family dynamics than many addicts. Mr. C had lied to his wife and family about his financial losses, loans, and employment issues and had refused to openly discuss myriad other issues with them. Within a matter of a few weeks, he became radically more open and self-disclosing in therapy and with his family. The patient called me one morning in crisis after a brief gambling relapse and reported that he was suicidal and could not live with himself and all the destruction he had created in all of their lives.

After this event, the patient continued in therapy, GA, and marital therapy, and his spouse and children also remained in treatment. He became more fully and honestly disclosing with his wife, eventually assumed a leadership role in the GA community, and once again became a successful businessman His family relationships improved dramatically, and very importantly, he has abstained from all gambling activities for over three years.

In part, the addiction process begins as a result of the inability to openly disclose and communicate about personal feelings, traumatic and difficult life realities, and even more simple matters. As the addiction process evolves, the addict or substance abuser becomes progressively and more pathologically self-centered (Adams, 2009). As indicated in chapter two (Jourard, 1964, 1968), one important etiological component in mental health problems and pathological adjustment styles is the inability to be self-disclosing with others. This same general premise pertains to the onset and progression of the addictive disorders.

During the middle and later stages of the active addiction process (Forrest, 1975, 1994, 2005, 2008), addicts self-disclose less and less. Addicts generally become more self-focused and addiction-focused as a part of the self-centeredness and pathological narcissism (Forrest, 1999) of any addictive disease. They become progressively less capable of open, healthy, self-disclosing behaviors. The malignant self-absorption, narcissism, and self-centeredness of the later stages of the addiction process progressively leads to self-destruction. At this juncture in the addiction process, the addicted person's avoidance defense system (Forrest, 1999, 2009) contributes greatly to the addict's inability to self-disclose. Denial, distortion, projection, repression, and the other primary defense mechanisms of the avoidance defense system make it progressively more difficult for the late stage addict to engage in self-disclosing behavior.

As the addict moves away from potentially healthy self-disclosing relationships with others and withdraws into self and the self-centeredness of the addiction process, he or she becomes sicker, more self-centered, and more self-destructive. At some point in this process, the addict is no longer physically or psychologically capable of establishing or maintaining drug abstinence in the absence of hospitalization, detoxication, or involvement in a residential care setting. The patient cannot begin to move toward and with others or begin the self-disclosing process of recovery at this point in the addiction process.

In short, most addicts appear to be people who have always experienced difficulties with interpersonal relationships (Forrest, 1985, 1999, 2002, 2006, 2009) and self-disclosing. An inability to self-disclose in a consistent and healthy manner is a precursor to the development of a wide array of maladaptive or parataxic behaviors including the addictive disorders. The addictive process always erodes an individual's capacity to self-disclose. As people progress into the middle and later stages of the active addiction process, they lose whatever prior abilities they had for healthy self-disclosure as well as functional and intimate human relationships. Floridly addicted late-stage alcoholics and addicts are destructively self-centered and nondisclosing. Most of these individuals seem to be incapable of healthy change, sustained drug abstinence, self-disclosure, and interpersonal growth in the absence of intensive professional and self-help treatment engagement.

SELF-DISCLOSURE AND THE ALCOHOLICS ANONYMOUS SELF-HELP RECOVERY MODEL

The recovery process is initiated vis-à-vis drug/addiction abstinence and maintained by the commitment to an ongoing program of recovery and change. Recovery also entails (Forrest, 1994, 1995; Adams, 2009) the death of the former addicted self and the rebirth of a new or recovering self. Indeed, there are a multiplicity of factors associated with the recovery process. Self-disclosure is also a key ingredient in the recovery process.

There may be many roads or paths to recovery and the recovery process, but after spending some thirty-five years treating thousands of addicts and substance abusers, it has been the author's observation that a number of common denominators seem to play crucial roles in the recoveries of most addicted persons. Most, if not all, of these common denominators in the recovery process are also central to the wisdom of Alcoholics Anonymous (AA) and the collective wisdom of the self-help community (Adams, 2009).

Many years ago (Forrest, 1975), I suggested that "the success of this organization (AA) is predicated upon teaching the alcoholic self-disclosing behaviors as well as simply more effective relating types of behavior." (p. 238) The essence of most AA and other self-help meetings has to do with communicative and relational sharing and telling others about one's self. This self-disclosure is very total, and is done in the absence of alcohol or other psychoactive substances. Within the confines of AA or other self-help meetings, addicts learn that they can "unload" and share the emotional and cognitive "crap" they have been repressing and denying for a lifetime, and be valued, nurtured, and loved in spite of all these painful realities and flaws. They also make friends and are accepted as human beings in the process. These transactions can be synergistic and help many addicts effect a radically changed lifestyle. An attempted movement toward and with others, which is based upon mutual self-disclosure and transparency, suddenly becomes the interpersonal modus operandi of many recovery addicts. The ever growing generalization of this process probably accounts for much of the success of AA and the self-help community over the past seventy-five years. Twelve-step work, helping others, and community service become the hallmark of many recovering people.

Self-disclosing and telling other addicts about one's self, direct and open helping relationships with other addicts, and sharing experiences, strengths, and wisdom with others facilitates the recovery process. Self-disclosure in recovery is paradoxically difficult and yet, once initiated and with sustained drug abstinence, becomes progressively easier and spontaneous.

To date, Alcoholics Anonymous and the self-help community (Adams, 2009) has been one of the most effective, if not *the* most effective, treatment alternative for alcoholics and other addicts. Narcotics Anonymous (NA), Cocaine Anonymous (CA), Overeaters Anonymous (OA) and the other off-shoots of AA are constructed around the twelve-steps and other basic literature, procedures, and precepts of Alcoholics Anonymous. Those familiar with the format, philosophical basis, and literature of AA understand and appreciate the relevance of self-disclosure to the success of this organization. Self-disclosure, being honest with oneself and others, admitting to being powerless over alcohol, making a searching and fearless moral inventory of oneself, and "admitting" to God, to oneself, and to another human being the exact nature of our wrongs all involve the essentials of self-disclosure. The more one evaluates and scrutinizes the underpinnings and basic precepts of AA, the clearer it becomes that self-disclosure is indeed a cornerstone of the AA program of recovery.

Alcoholics Anonymous (1976) is constructed around the following twelve-steps of recovery. The self-disclosure aspects of the AA twelve-step recovery program will be briefly discussed. "Here are the (AA) steps we took which are suggested as a program of recovery. We:

(1) "ADMITTED WE WERE POWERLESS OVER ALCOHOL—THAT OUR LIVES HAD BECOME UNMANAGEABLE." "Admitted" in the

context of this sentence implies self-disclosure of one's alcohol dependence and related unmanageable life. This step initially involves admitting to oneself the reality of being powerless over alcohol and also implies eventual admission of this reality to others. And admission of any self-related reality can be a very powerful form of self-disclosure.

(2) "CAME TO BELIEVE THAT A POWER GREATER THAT OURSELVES COULD RESTORE US TO SANITY." This step covertly involves the self-disclosure that one's alcoholism or alcoholic behavior is "insane." The alcoholic, in effect, acknowledges that he or she has become insane by taking this step. Further reflection on this matter after establishing alcohol and drug abstinence usually fosters the recovering person's awareness of just how crazy, out-of-control, insane, and unmanageable his or her life had become via the addiction process. It is terribly difficult to admit to self or others that one has become insane or out of control. It can be even more difficult to disclose these realities to others. And yet, these disclosures can help initiate and sustain the recovery process.

(3) "MADE A DECISION TO TURN OUR WILL AND OUR LIVES OVER TO THE CARE OF GOD AS WE UNDERSTOOD HIM." Taking this step requires the alcoholic to self-disclose to God, a higher power, and eventually others that he or she has decided to turn his or her life over to a being, power, or source greater than self. In effect, by taking this step, the recovering person discloses "I am unable to manage or control my alcoholism and life, and I am turning to God or another source for help. Taking step three is also an important covert disclosure that helps initiate the recovering person's growth beyond the self-centeredness and pathological narcissism that has historically governed the active alcoholic process.

(4) "MADE A SEARCHING AND FEARLESS MORAL INVENTORY OF OURSELVES." While this step initially appears to be unrelated to self-disclosure, anyone who has ever attempted to take a sincere and in-depth moral examination or self-evaluation realizes that such a process can only begin and be conducted via authentic, honest, and in-depth self-disclosure. Self-talk, self-examination, and thus "a searching and fearless moral inventory of ourselves" begins and is accomplished by an honest, thorough, and authentic disclosing of the self to oneself. "Getting honest" with oneself is at the core of the recovery process, and this can only be accomplished by developing the capacity for honest self-disclosing.

(5) "ADMITTED TO GOD, TO OURSELVES, AND TO ANOTHER HUMAN BEING THE EXACT NATURE OF OUR WRONGS." "Admitted" in the context of step five refers explicitly to self-disclosing to God, self, and another human being the "exact" nature of the alcoholic's "wrongs." This step calls for an exact and full self-disclosure of the person's wrongs to God, self, and at least one other human being. For many recovering alcoholics,

self-disclosure to another human being takes place within the context of a sponsorship relationship. For others, full self-disclosure pertaining to these matters may take place between the recovering person and his of her therapist, counselor, or significant other. It is significant that the wisdom of the AA program is perhaps most exemplified in the requirement of this step that full self-disclosure needs to be made to another human being. The cathartic, confessional, and relational aspects of the alcoholic's self-disclosure in this specific realm foster the potential for interpersonal and intrapersonal growth, change, and recovery.

(6) "WERE ENTIRELY READY TO HAVE GOD REMOVE ALL THESE DEFECTS OF CHARACTER." By disclosing the exact nature of his of her wrongs, the alcoholic simultaneously acknowledges and self-discloses these "defects of character." This step implies a personal readiness and belief that God or a power greater than self can remove character defects or simply help the recovering person change dysfunctional behaviors, thoughts, and emotions. Acknowledging and self-disclosing personal defects is also central to the process of becoming ready to have God remove character defects as well as enhancing the capacity and readiness for assuming greater personal responsibility for healthy growth and character change.

(7) "HUMBLY ASKED HIM TO REMOVE OUR SHORTCOMINGS." The disclosure of personal flaws, inadequacies, and shortcomings is prerequisite to the recovering person's ability to humbly ask for help or assistance with the removal of personal conflicts. "Asking" for any form of help or assistance always begins with the personal disclosure of shortcomings, behaviors, or sources of conflict. The alcoholic "humbly" asks for assistance as he or she discloses personal shortcomings as this approach makes it easier to self-disclose in a more fully open, honest, sensitive, and non self-centered, arrogant, or demanding manner.

(8) "MADE A LIST OF ALL PERSONS WE HAD HARMED AND BECAME WILLING TO MAKE AMENDS TO THEM ALL." This is an action and preparation for initiating change. Taking this step requires that the recovering person be ready and willing to openly self-disclose via the process of making amends to those he or she has harmed.

(9) "MADE DIRECT AMENDS TO SUCH PEOPLE WHEREVER POSSIBLE." This step is based upon all of the self-disclosures that were central to and are now required to make amends to others who have been hurt and harmed. It is impossible to make direct amends to others in the absence of self-disclosing, acknowledging, and communicating openly and honestly with those who have been harmed. The actions and sources of harm are again self-disclosed to both self and others. In short, making direct amends wherever possible involves self-disclosing to others who have been harmed wherever possible!

(10) "CONTINUED TO TAKE PERSONAL INVENTORY AND WHEN WE WERE WRONG PROMPTLY ADMITTED IT." By continuing to take a personal inventory, the recovering person must also continue to make self-disclosures to himself or herself. These continuing self-disclosures and self-dialogues need to be based on rigorous honesty and reality. This step also stipulates that the recovering person promptly "admit" when he or she has been wrong. Again, admissions are based almost solely upon the communicative mechanism of self-disclosure. This step encompasses acknowledging and self-disclosing these wrongs to both self and others.

(11) "SOUGHT THROUGH PRAYER AND MEDITATION TO IMPROVE OUR CONSCIOUS CONTACT WITH GOD 'AS WE UNDERSTAND HIM,' PRAYING ONLY FOR KNOWLEDGE OF HIS WILL FOR US AND THE POWER TO CARRY THAT OUT." Both prayer and meditation involve self-disclosure. Prayer may include disclosing one's problems and difficulties in life to God or a "higher power." Prayer also can include admitting and disclosing personal wrongs and asking for forgiveness or guidance. Prayer is often steeped in self-disclosing behavior. Meditation may involve deep and focused self-thought and intimate self-disclosures. Self-disclosure via the mediums of meditation and prayer foster conscious contact with God or a higher power and may also be key to developing a sense of knowledge of His will for the recovering person as well as the strength and power to carry out this process.

(12) "HAVING HAD A SPIRITUAL AWAKENING AS A RESULT OF THESE STEPS, WE TRIED TO CARRY THIS MESSAGE TO ALCOHOLICS AND PRACTICE IT IN ALL OUR AFFAIRS." It has been my consistent observation based upon psychotherapeutic work with thousands of alcoholics that a "spiritual awakening" can take place as a result of taking and consistently "working" these steps. Any effort to carry this message to other alcoholics relies heavily upon personal self-disclosures and ultimately can only occur via open communication and self-disclosure. Practicing this message in all our affairs also requires practicing ongoing self-disclosures, openness, and honesty with self and others.

The twelve-steps of Alcoholics Anonymous (1976, pp. 58–60) and all other twelve-step based recovery programs (NA, OA, CA, GA, etc.) are self-disclosure oriented and based. While the self-disclosure dimension of the twelve-step recovery programs (Adams, 2009) is but one facet of this general recovery model, it is an important ingredient in the success of all self-help recovery programs. Twelve-step recovery alternatives are action-oriented, cognitive-behavioral, spiritual, interpersonal and intrapersonal, supportive and nurturing, and self-disclosure based. Alcoholics Anonymous is a therapeutic organization and community.

The 'HOW IT WORKS' chapter in the Alcoholics Anonymous "Big Book" addresses a variety of issues associated with the nature of alcoholism and alcoholics, necessities or prerequisites to recovery, and how AA works:

> Rarely have we seen a person fail who has thoroughly followed our path. Those who do not are people who cannot or will not completely give themselves to this simple program, usually men and women who are constitutionally incapable of being honest with themselves. There are such unfortunates. They are not at fault; they seem to have been born that way. They are naturally incapable of grasping and developing a manner of living which demands "rigorous honesty." Their chances are less than average. There are those, too, who suffer from grave emotional and mental disorders, but many of them do recover if they have the capacity to be honest.
>
> Our stories "disclose" in a general way what we used to be like, what happened and what we are like now. If you have decided you want what we have and are willing to go to any length to get it—then you are ready to take certain steps.
>
> At some of these we balked. We thought we could find an easier, softer way. But we could not. With all the earnestness at our command, we beg of you to be fearless and thorough from the very start. Some of us have tried to hold on to our old ideas and the result was nil until we let go absolutely.
>
> Remember that we deal with alcohol, cunning, baffling and powerful! Without help it is too much for us. But there is One who has all power—that One is God. May you find Him now.
>
> Half measures availed us nothing. We stood at the turning point. We asked for His protection with care and complete abandon.
>
> Here are the steps (twelve-steps) we took which are "suggested as a program of recovery. (pp. 58–60)

The "Little Red Book" (Forrest, 1994) and other AA publications consistently stress the importance of being rigorously honest with self, God, and "fellow man" as the cornerstone in the AA bridge to recovery and sobriety: "Without honesty the AA program would become an inconsistent, hypocritical way of life. It would become negative and antagonistic to recovery. The practice of dishonesty in any form helps to tear down the alcoholic's defense against that first drink which he will eventually find himself taking, if he cannot be honest with himself" (p. 117).

The fellowship and healthy interpersonal relatedness of AA and the self-help community is also essential to the success of the recovery program. The therapeutic vicissitudes of self-disclosure, honesty, commitment to the AA program, and a willingness to change patterns of thinking and behavior are essential to recovery. The AA community also acknowledges the role and difficulties that mental disorders and severe emotional problems present for many alcoholics and addicts. Nonetheless, the self-help community provides the hope of recovery for many people who manifest co-occurring psychiatric illness and emotional disturbance. The AA program of recovery recommends that members who are unable to overcome uncontrollable fears and other emotional difficulties seek medical and psychiatric help.

Alcoholics Anonymous and the self-help community (Adams, 2009) is more than an organization of people who have committed themselves to alcohol and drug abstinence and the recovery process. Rather, AA and the other self-help recovery alternatives (OA, GA, CA, NA) represent an alternative lifestyle and philosophical approach to the process of daily living. Recovery, drug abstinence, personality growth and change, and self-disclosure are central to this more healthy approach to human living.

SELF-DISCLOSURE AND RECOVERY FROM PSYCHOLOGICAL PROBLEMS AND PSYCHIATRIC DISORDERS

Virtually all psychiatric illnesses and disorders are subject to positive change. Partial and full recoveries from even the most severe psychiatric disorders do occur. A diversity of mild to moderate psychological problems can also be effectively treated by psychotherapy, medication, self-help treatments, and/or a combination of these modalities. Many emotional difficulties and less severe psychological disorders spontaneously remit with the passage of time (Eysenck, 1965; Forrest, 1997; Norcross, 2002; Truax and Carkhuff, 1967).

Self-disclosure is an important ingredient in the recovery from both mild psychological problems and severe psychiatric illness. The theoretical, clinical, and research underpinnings of this position were elucidated in chapter two through four of this text. People who experience mild to moderate anxiety, irrational fears, dysthymia or situational depression, marital discord, grief and loss, emotional distress associated with job loss or divorce, stress, sleep problems, and any number of other psychological problems can recover fully or partially from the various conflicts and symptoms that accompany these disorders. Recovery from any of these psychological problems often begins with self-disclosing to a counselor, family member, friend, physician, or significant other about resultant symptoms, causes, and other matters pertaining to the affected person's psychological problems or disorder.

Patient openness and self-disclosure is also essential to the process of recovery or partial-recovery from a major psychiatric illness. The discovery and eventual diagnosis of schizophrenia often occurs vis-à-vis the self-disclosures that pre-schizophrenic adolescents make to their parents, significant others, or family physicians. Effective interventions in schizophrenia take place when adolescents and young adults begin to openly disclose their confused thoughts, hallucinations and delusions, and bizarre beliefs to a parent. Parental or therapist disclosures to psychiatrists and other clinicians may synergize the treatment and recovery process for these individuals. Eventually the reciprocal disclosures of all involved in the treatment and recovery process further potentiates the recovery process. Intervention, treatment, and the recovery process for bipolar illness, schizo-affective illness and other major mental illnesses also tend to hinge upon the patient's self-disclosures.

Human beings rely upon self-disclosure to obtain help and care for their illnesses and problems. Medical patients must disclose their symptoms and condition to physicians or other health care specialists in order to help these professionals understand, diagnose, provide appropriate treatments, and eventually help them recover. Psychotherapy and psychiatric patients also must disclose their various conflicts, symptoms, feelings, and thoughts in order to obtain appropriate and effective care. The families and loved ones of emotionally conflicted or severely mentally ill people can also play important roles in the recovery from psychiatric illness (De Quardo, 2006). The personal self-disclosures that parents and significant others share with psychiatrists, psychologists, and counselors about their emotionally disturbed or mentally ill family members can be crucial to establishing an accurate diagnosis and providing proper care for these persons.

Self-disclosure and openness about emotional problems and psychiatric illness or symptoms is generally far more prevalent and socially acceptable today than thirty to over one hundred years ago. And yet, even today many people in many different cultures and societies continue to be very non-disclosing, avoidant, and secretive about emotional and psychological problems. In America and most Western cultures, it is now (Forrest, 2007, 2009) clearly recognized and accepted that openness and self-disclosure about one's emotional and psychiatric problems is almost always an essential precursor to the process of obtaining effective care, changing or returning to emotional health, and recovery.

Thousands of research and clinical publications have been produced over the past one hundred years that document the recoveries and changes people with every form of psychological and psychiatric illness or disorder have experienced. Recent (Bruni, 2006; Macphee, 2004) non-clinical and nonscientific publications also address the issue of recovery from schizophrenia and major mental illness. These publications often include articles and case studies by professional mental health workers, but they also include personal recovery and treatment accounts and stories by people who have struggled with major mental illness and various psychiatric disorders. Most of these publications and articles (*Schizophrenia Digest*, 2004) are steeped in self-disclosure. The authors frequently go into great depth and detail about their personal experiences with not only mental illness and psychiatric disturbance, but also with family and social dynamics, diagnostic issues, treatment experiences, social stigma, and the struggle to change and recover. A theme in this recovery-oriented literature is simply that persons who manifest a diversity of very serious psychological and psychiatric disorders can change and experience varying levels or types of recovery. As Roberts (2004) emphasizes, many debilitating forms of mental illness such as schizophrenia are accompanied by a co-occurring substance use disorder.

In short, self-disclosure is an essential and multidimensional component in the recovery from a diversity of psychological and psychiatric disorders. The following case vignettes demonstrate the importance of the roles of self-disclosure in recovery from different emotional or psychiatric disorders.

Case 1: Willard A., a forty-six-year-old single male, was recently referred to the author following a brief psychiatric hospitalization for alcohol detoxification. During the initial session, Mr. A. indicated that he had been medically and psychiatrically hospitalized one or two times a month for over five years and he was unable to work and had been on disability for nearly fifteen years. He readily disclosed his various psychiatric and medical diagnoses which included bipolar illness, social anxiety disorder, alcohol dependence, panic disorder, esophageal and gastrointestinal hemorrhaging, a "bad back," obesity, and elevated blood pressure. He also disclosed that he had been consuming between twelve and twenty-four beers daily throughout the course of his fifteen years of ongoing psychiatric and medical care. He disclosed that his treatment had been limited to psychiatric visits for medication and ongoing medical care and brief hospitalizations for many years. The client had never been involved in residential treatment, intensive individual psychotherapy, family therapy, self-help treatment, or a monitored antabuse maintenance program. Based upon these self-disclosures, I immediately had the client sign appropriate release of information forms and contacted his parents, psychiatrist, family physician, and the local mental health center to obtain the proper paper work to get Mr. A. admitted to a long-term (ninety day) residential program at the state hospital for "dual-diagnosis" patients.

Within a matter of weeks, Mr. A. was admitted to this intensive, structured, and long-term program for patients with severe psychiatric illness and a concurrent substance use disorder. Willard's local psychiatrist had to withdraw him from Klonopin prior to admission, his medications were changed during the course of residential care, he initiated self-help treatment, and was seen in monthly individual psychotherapy after release from residential care. Involvement with vocational rehabilitation resulted in a part-time job, and the patient has remained totally alcohol abstinent and in treatment for over two years. The client has never been psychiatrically or medically hospitalized since. He has also lost over sixty pounds and is no longer socially phobic and has experienced no further anxiety/panic attacks or episodes of discontinuing his bipolar medications. Mr. A. has been employed on a fifteen to twenty hours per week basis for some fourteen months.

The client's early self-disclosures in therapy pertaining to his clinical history and general lack of appropriate care facilitated the initiation and maintenance of more adequate and appropriate treatment interventions, which fostered a rather quick and very significant recovery upon the part of Mr. A.

Case 2: Mary N. was a forty-two-year-old single woman. She was referred to the author by a local psychiatric hospital following a brief inpatient stay for stabilization. The client disclosed that she was a "paranoid schizophrenic" and had discontinued her psychotropic medication and initiated heavy drinking for two or three weeks prior to her psychiatric hospitalization. She was also unemployed and involved in a complicated sexual relationship. Mrs. N. had completed an undergraduate degree in psychology as well as a master's degree in counseling, and she was a licensed professional counselor (LPC) as well as a certified addictions counselor. The client openly disclosed her protracted clinical history of remaining alcohol free for several months and then "binge drinking" for a few days or weeks, discontinuing her medications, and ending up in the hospital for a few days. Mary reported that this cycle had reoccurred for ten years. She had seen a number of therapists briefly and had infrequently attended self-help meetings over the years, but had been unable to sustain an ongoing psychotherapy relationship or consistent and active self-help engagement. She had sustained a relationship with a psychiatrist for over three years and saw him for medication management each three or four months or when she needed to be psychiatrically hospitalized.

This client was seen in individual psychotherapy on a weekly or every other week basis for sixteen months. She also began attending a women's AA group each week, and eventually became employed in a part-time program administration position at a local mental health center. She took antabuse three times per week for six months and remained on her prescribed psychotropic medications during the course of her therapeutic involvement. She has not required further psychiatric hospitalization or alcohol use related care in over four years.

Basic client and therapist self-disclosures pertaining to the client's prior diagnoses, clinical history, and treatment/self-help case histories were central to initiating the various changes that positively impacted her recovery and life.

Case 3: Jimmy J., a fifteen-year-old adolescent, was seen for consultation and brief family therapy following an incident that involved marijuana "experimentation" and school expulsion. Jimmy very quickly explained to the therapist that "pot" helped him "relax and mellow out." His parents disclosed in the initial family therapy session that Jimmy was "up most of the night; his room is totally disorganized and a wreck," and they were concerned about his "strange behaviors." They also "suspected" that Jimmy had been smoking pot and involved in other drugs for over two years. All agreed that he was tired, fatigued, depressed, disheveled, confused at times, and unable to function socially and in school. His parents were also concerned that he was involved with selling drugs. They were also fearful that he would "end up in jail." Jimmy additionally disclosed to the author in the initial two or three individual therapy sessions that he had been experiencing severe headaches, loss of appetite, and an upset stomach for a few months. He felt "lifted" when he smoked marijuana, which in truth, he had been smoking several times a day for nearly two years.

These patient and familial self-disclosures formed the basis for the author's repetitive recommendation that Jimmy be seen by a medical doctor and eventually by a neurologist. Nearly three months after the patient was initially seen for therapy and consultation, he was seen by a neurologist and completed an MRI and an extensive neurological workup. The client died from an inoperable brain tumor thirteen months later.

Again, these case studies elucidate the relevance and importance of client self-disclosures in accurately assessing and treating a diversity of behavioral health and addictive disorders. Honest client self-disclosures are of paramount importance to the clinician's role in diagnosing and providing appropriate treatments for people. Chemically dependant and addicted clients are notorious for denying, lying, minimizing, and obfuscating their symptoms and conflicts. Thus, it is always incumbent upon therapists to actively, supportively, and consistently encourage these clients to practice openness and honesty within the context of the therapeutic relationship and with other health providers. Recovery can only begin and develop vis-à-vis the client's enhanced capacity for engaging in more open, honest, and healthy self-disclosing forms of communication.

SUMMARY

The inability to self-disclose in a consistent, healthy, and optimal manner is a core psychological-interpersonal ingredient in the etiology of virtually all addictive disorders. The author's extensive experience pertaining to this aspect of the addiction process was examined early in this chapter. Most people who eventually recover or are "recovering" from a diversity of addictive disorders develop a very obvious capacity for increased openness, authenticity, and self-disclosure. Case studies involving a compulsive gambler,

Chapter 7

Therapist and Client Self-Disclosure in Chemical Dependency Counseling

INTRODUCTION

Chapters 2 and 4 examined the theoretical and research evidence pertaining to self-disclosure in counseling and psychotherapy as well as the effects of therapist and client self-disclosure in psychotherapy. As noted in these chapters, the research and clinical practice literature pertaining to self-disclosure in psychotherapy is limited. The literature pertaining to the realm of therapist and client self-disclosure in chemical dependency counseling and addictions treatment is even more limited; however, empirical data and clinical information pertaining to this specific topic was also discussed in these earlier chapters.

This chapter addresses many of the important clinical and therapeutic aspects of self-disclosure in the specific realm of chemical dependency counseling. Self-disclosure issues pertaining to therapist and client beliefs about the etiology or causative factors associated with chemical dependency and the addictive disorders are briefly addressed in this chapter. The impact, dynamics, and various effects of client and therapist self-disclosures related to the diagnostic process in chemical dependency counseling are also discussed in the chapter. Finally, this chapter examines the therapeutic and potentially iatrogenic impact and effects of client and therapist self-disclosures upon the process and outcome of counseling relationships with chemically dependent persons. A number of brief case studies and actual therapy vignettes are also included in the chapter. These case studies and therapy vignettes demonstrate how client and therapist self-disclosures impact all aspects and stages of diagnostic and therapeutic work with this clinical population.

A good deal of the material presented in this chapter focuses upon the process of intensive individual counseling and psychotherapy work with alcoholics and other chemically dependent clients. The author has written extensively about the process of intensive psychotherapy with chemically dependent persons (Forrest, 1985, 1992, 1994, 1995, 1997, 1999, 2002), and a review of some of these publications may help readers more fully appreciate the impact and scope of self-disclosure in therapeutic relationships with this population.

THERAPIST AND CLIENT SELF-DISCLOSURE AND THE ISSUE OF ETIOLOGY IN CHEMICAL DEPENDENCY COUNSELING

Therapists manifest a diversity of beliefs, attitudes, and precepts pertaining to the cause or origins of chemical dependency. Researchers and clinicians (Forrest, 1978, 1985, 1999; Shaffer, 2006; Wanner et al., 2009) have developed numerous theories and etiologic models of addiction and chemical dependency. All of these models have, in effect, been based upon the self-disclosures of literally millions of people who have developed addictions and/or chemical dependency problems. Therapists and researchers (Shaffer, 2006) have interviewed clients and family members; conducted psychological testing, evaluations, and medical tests; and reviewed educational, religious, cultural, socioeconomic, racial, and various other sources of data pertaining to hundreds of thousands of chemically dependent and addicted persons. Client self-disclosures have formed the basis for constructing cognitive-behavioral, genetic and familial, sociologic, learning theory, disease, psychodynamic and analytic, and other science-based models or etiological explanations of addictive behaviors and chemical dependency. Even non-science based explanations or models of addictive behavior are related to the self-disclosures of the people who manifest these behaviors. For example, religions or biblical explanations of alcoholism were developed via the self-disclosures and behaviors of biblical figures over two thousand years ago.

Recent etiological models of chemical dependency (Forrest 1999; Skeel et al., 2008; Shaffer et al., 2004; Shaffer, 2006; Stein, Dixon and Nyamathi, 2008) are multivariate and/or syndrome-oriented models. These models are far more complex, sophisticated, and science based than the more simple univariant models of the not too distant past (Blane, 1968; Blane and Leonard, 1987; Forrest, 1997). Nonetheless, a diversity of client-based self-disclosures always determines or impacts the nature and roles of a wide variety of etiologic variables that contribute to syndrome and multivariate models or explanations of addictions and the substance use disorders.

Therapist and clinician self-disclosure have also played a central role in the evolution of etiological models of the addictions. Therapists and clinicians have discussed their beliefs and clinical experiences related to the causes of their client's addictive behaviors and conflicts for well over one hundred years. Therapists unendingly and ethically disclose about their clinical experiences and theoretical models of the addictions with professional colleagues, their clients, and the general public. Thousands of books and clinical publications as well as millions of radio, TV, newspaper, and other media sources address the causes and nature of addictive behaviors on a daily basis. Most of these sources of general information pertaining to the addictions come from the various disclosures of clinicians, researchers, or recovering addicts and substance abusers.

In short, the various etiological models of addictions and addictive behaviors have been constructed around the self-disclosures of patients or clients as well as therapists and health care providers. Even the most modern "hard science" based assessment modalities that are used to diagnose alcoholism and the addictions rely upon patient and clinician self-disclosures. Blood studies, MRI's, CT and PET scans, and other medical assessments and diagnostic tools rely upon the biophysiologic disclosures of the patient. Psychological test results and clinical assessments of chemically dependent and addictive persons are in many respects determined by the self-disclosures of patients. As health care providers and patients have interactively self-disclosed their beliefs, opinions, and clinical and research findings with each other and the general public, a diversity of etiologic or causative models and explanations of addictive behavior and chemical dependency have been developed. Self-disclosure continues to play a multiplicity of crucial roles in the evolution of our understanding of all addictions.

SELF-DISCLOSURE AND DIFFERENTIAL DIAGNOSIS IN CHEMICAL DEPENDENCY COUNSELING

While the role of diagnosis remains somewhat controversial in the treatment of psychiatric and psychological disorders as well as the addictions and chemical dependency, most clinicians and behavioral health providers agree that an accurate diagnosis or differential diagnosis forms the basis or cornerstone for providing appropriate, efficacious, and evidence-based treatment interventions for their patients (Forrest, 1994, 1997, 2009; Dillon, 2006).

As noted in chapter 6, therapists and clinicians must rely upon the honest and forthright self-disclosures of their substance-abusing or chemically dependent clients in order to provide accurate diagnoses and appropriate treatments for these persons. Many or perhaps most chemically dependent persons do not initially provide therapists and clinicians with honest and full disclosures pertaining to their alcohol and drug use as well as the various other facets of their lives. These clients are especially notorious (Bratter and Forrest, 1985; Forrest, 1978, 2002, 2007) for their capacity to minimize or deny personal conflicts. They also may lie to therapists and others or be prone to telling "half truths." The distortions, deceptions, and propensity for simply not telling clinicians the truth are factors that sometimes severely impede the therapist's ability to successfully diagnose and treat chemically dependent persons.

The diagnostic process begins when clients enter the therapist's office and begin to interact and communicate with a secretary or other administrative personnel and eventually the therapist. Physical appearance and dress, verbal interactions and communication style, eye contact, and literally every facet of the client's behavior ultimately provides the skilled clinician with disclosures and grist for the diagnostic process.

Within the context of the actual therapist-client clinical diagnostic interviewing process, it is very important for the therapist to openly emphasize and consistently stress the importance of the client's openness, full disclosures, and honest reporting of personal information. This technique will generally facilitate more honest, open, and forthright self-disclosing behaviors upon the part of many chemically dependent persons. Therapists and clinicians also need to openly disclose to clients very early in the assessment process. Therapists initially disclose about their treatment interventions, treatment plans, training and education, and capacity to effectively help the client. Therapists explain to clients that they will be limited or adversely impacted by the client's half-truths, lies, denial, limited self-disclosures, dishonesty, and resistance to openness and full participation in the diagnostic process as well as the treatment process. Skilled and experienced chemical dependency counselors (Forrest, 1978, 1994, 2002, 2009) usually realize that the vast majority of chemically dependent clients and addicts need to establish and sustain several months or perhaps even years of drug abstinence, active treatment engagement, and recovery before they develop the capacity for a full, open, and honest self-disclosing adjustment style. Nonetheless, these initial therapist strategies enhance the probability that chemically dependent clients will generally be more open, honest, and disclosing during the diagnostic and assessment stage of treatment.

The diagnostic process is not static. It is a continually changing and evolving process. It is of paramount importance for the therapist (Forrest, 1985, 1994, 1997, 2008) to openly disclose and fully discuss his or her diagnostic findings and impressions with the client. This therapist technique models honesty and openness, self-disclosing behavior, and genuineness to the client. The feedback and responses of the client to the therapist's early disclosures pertaining to the client's diagnostic status provide the therapist with a better understanding of the client's readiness and motivation for treatment engagement, level of denial and resistance to change, and various other intrapersonal and relational dynamics.

Reciprocal and mutual self-disclosures between the therapist and client during the clinical interviewing and diagnostic assessment stages of treatment contribute significantly to the development and maintenance of a working and productive therapeutic alliance (Forrest, 1994, 1997, 2009). Therapist and client self-disclosures are central to the process of accurately diagnosing and eventually providing appropriate and efficacious treatments for all substance-abusing and chemically dependent persons.

The following individual psychotherapy vignette demonstrates some of the roles, therapeutic issues, and importance of therapist as well as client self-disclosures during the initial diagnostic and therapeutic stages of work with a twenty-one year-old alcohol dependent client:

Bart C: Yeah, I'd like to cut back on my drinking, or maybe quit for awhile . . . I know I need to at least cut back.

Doctor F: I know we've only met three times, but it seems to me that you've continued to experience some really scary consequences as a result of your drinking over the past three weeks . . . I mean a DUI, having to leave college, and now ending up in an ICU and getting eight teeth knocked out . . . plus a fractured jaw . . . do you think that maybe you need to stop drinking completely, and try to make a one-day-at-a-time commitment to total abstinence?

Bart C: I know it looks bad for me, Doc, but I know I can cut back . . . I've done it a lot of times . . . I never drank during football season when I was in high school, and it was a piece of cake . . . I quit for a few weeks my freshman year at college after I got the underage drinking ticket, and that was a piece of cake too . . . I know I can do it, and my parents are just over-concerned . . . ha, ha . . . it sounds like you are too, and I'm the only one payin' the price . . . My damned mouth and jaw still hurt like hell and I've lost my million dollar grin . . . at least until I get my new front teeth!

Doctor F: Do you remember us discussing my concerns about your trying to control your drinking two weeks ago . . . Your test results, the MAC-R score and your MMPI-II test results indicating that you may have alcoholism . . . Your test results tell me that you need to stop drinking completely, plus Dr. Lewis's call about your medical tests . . . your liver enzymes being really elevated . . . I think you've been honest with me about drinking fifteen to twenty beers on most days for the past two or three years, and that's why I wanted you and your folks to consider inpatient treatment of at least an IOP and maybe a few days of detox care.

Bart C: But I have stopped for a few days . . . I guess being in the ICU and the hospital for a few days probably helped me detox, but I don't want to drink now . . . hell, getting run over on my bicycle the other night about killed me, and I sure don't want to die . . . Ha. . . . Ha . . . Plus, I've got to get a job, and I want to get my car back . . . I've got to take those DUI classes, and I don't even know how I'll get there without a driver's license and a car.

Doctor F: That's part of the stuff that concerns me, Bart. And I know your parents are really worried about your life . . . you had a BAC of .26 when you got the DUI, and your dad said your BAC at the hospital last week after you got hit was a .32 . . . that was at 3:30 a.m. . . . Can you see why we're all concerned and trying to get you to make a commitment to abstinence or inpatient care, or a more intensive treatment regimen?

Bart C: Yeah, I know you're all worried about me, Doc . . . my little sister is even more worried about me too, and I'm really close to her . . . and I've tried to tell you everything, Doc . . . not like the other counselors in the past . . . hell, I've been to five or six different therapists since I was thirteen or fourteen . . . Not for drinking or the pot, but like I told you when I first came in here . . . for the other shit . . . stealing money from my parents, lying to them, and other stuff . . . I've never really been to jail yet, and I've never hurt anybody either . . . except my folks and myself, but I know deep down that I do have a drinking problem . . . At least I can admit that now.

Doctor F: I appreciate your openness with me, Bart, and your honesty about your drinking and the past. And we all agree that you have a drinking problem, but we've got some different ideas about treatment options, and I've also tried to be open with you about my experiences and opinions on these issues. Plus, it's got to be difficult for you to accept the reality that you can't beat this thing on your own, or it hasn't just stopped causing problems in your life . . . uh, your drinking.

Bart C: What do you mean? I guess I'm not understanding what you're saying, Doc.

Doctor F: Your alcoholism, Bart. I'm just saying that it's got to be difficult for any twenty-one year-old person, or anybody at any age for that matter, to begin to come to grips with or accept the reality that he or she has alcoholism . . . or a very severe drinking problem.

This therapy vignette demonstrates how the therapist openly and honestly shares his or her diagnostic impressions with the client early and throughout the diagnostic process. It is important for the therapist to be open and disclosing with clients even when he or she is not absolutely sure about a specific diagnosis. It is especially important for therapists to actively encourage clients to be honest and as fully self-disclosing as possible about their clinical histories and symptoms so that the therapist can provide more accurate diagnoses and more appropriate treatment interventions. The therapist attempts to initiate a working and productive alliance with the client during the diagnostic phase of treatment. This alliance or relationship will carry over to the actually therapeutic phase of care. The therapist-client diagnostic alliance is based upon mutual honesty, authenticity, openness, and self-disclosure, and it forms the cornerstone of every working and productive psychotherapeutic alliance or relationship (Forrest, 1994, 1999, 2009).

Chemically dependent and substance abusing persons manifest a diversity of symptoms and conflicts. Many of these individuals are diagnosed with severe personality disorders, affective disturbance, neurologic complications, anxiety disorders, and/or even major psychiatric illness (De Quardo, 2006; Fleming, 2009; Jewitt, 2006).

The following case study demonstrates the importance of client self-disclosure in co-occurring chemical dependency and major psychiatric disturbance.

Case 1: Carl W.'s mother contacted the author and scheduled a consultation session for her forty-one-year-old son. Mrs. W. initially reported by phone that her son was a "cocaine addict." She also noted that Carl had experienced "a lot of legal problems in the past."

Carl openly acknowledged that he had recently been hospitalized for psychiatric care on two occasions following two to three day cocaine "runs" that had resulted in acute depression and suicidal impulses. Carl also indicated during the initial consultation session that he had been incarcerated for fifteen years and was currently on parole. The client had been incarcerated on four different occasions. He was released from prison some six weeks before his initial session with the author, and he reportedly had been "doing cocaine" almost continuously since being released from the department of corrections. Mr. W. was also facing "the bitch" (the possibility of returning to prison "for life") if he was convicted of another felony. He expressed fear and concern to the author about "catching the bitch" (i.e., a habitual criminal offender conviction) and also repeatedly acknowledged that his cocaine addiction and his behavior were "insane."

Mr. W. had never been actively involved in self-help recovery, and he had never initiated psychiatric, substance abuse, or mental health care while incarcerated. However, he did agree to begin CA or AA and actually made an appointment with a psychiatrist after a few sessions with the author. He was diagnosed with major depression and "possible bipolar illness" by his psychiatrist and began taking psychotropic medication for his depressive disorder. Following three brief cocaine binges, Mr. W. entered a long-term (three month) dual-diagnosis residential treatment program. He then lived in a half-way house and was actively employed for six months.

As these programs were located in another state, the client was not seen by the author in individual therapy for nearly one year. However, upon returning to the Colorado Springs community, Carl re-engaged in therapy and was seen one to two times per month for over a year. He continued to be active in AA and CA (with ongoing sponsorship), remained drug free, saw his psychiatrist infrequently for medication management, and established full-time employment in the restaurant industry. He experienced no further legal difficulties and has sustained his recovery for nearly four years.

Carl and his mother's disclosures to the author very early in psychotherapy pertaining to cocaine dependence, mood regulation, and legal/antisocial difficulties were of paramount importance to the process of assessing and subsequently assisting with his appropriate care. Mr. W. did not manifest bipolar illness. He was treated for depression but his bipolar-like symptoms were the result of frequent cocaine "binges" and cocaine dependence. His general affective state stabilized following several months of cocaine abstinence. However, he continued to experience dysthymia following successful drug treatment. The client also manifested a mixed personality disorder with impulsive, antisocial, narcissistic, and OCD features. Based upon the client's overall clinical history, psychological test results, and his protracted history of incarceration and personality dysfunction, he was referred to a long-term residential treatment program that provided intensive care for "dually-diagnosed" offenders. Mr. W. was then transitioned back to the author for continued intensive individual psychotherapy and a more traditional outpatient treatment regimen for drug-dependent persons who manifest a multiplicity of rather severe psychological and social problems.

Patient, family member, and therapist/treatment provider self-disclosures played a key role in the diagnosis and successful ongoing treatment of Mr. W.

Psychological tests (Forrest, 1978, 1984, 1999, 2009) and medical tests (Forrest, 1997, 2006, 2008) can be very useful in the diagnosis of chemical dependency and addictive disorders as well as psychiatric disorders. Client or patient self-disclosure and honesty are essential to the therapist's optimal utilization of psychological testing results in diagnosing chemical dependency and psychological disorders. Therapist openness and the appropriate disclosure of test results is also an important component of diagnostic and treatment work with drug dependent, substance abusing, and emotionally conflicted persons.

The following therapy vignette illustrates some of the uses and dynamics of self-disclosure related to psychological testing in the differential diagnosis and psychotherapy of chemical dependency.

Doctor F: The first thing of importance about your test results (MMPI-II) is that you had a valid profile, Mary . . . I mean, you basically told the truth or were honest in your responses . . . I'll go over the results with you, and we'll see how accurate you think it is . . . if you feel the results fit you?

Mary: I'm glad to hear that it's valid . . . I tried to be honest, but that's a long test and it asked the same questions more than once.

Doctor F: Yeah, like we discussed prior to taking the test, it has scales that help me know if you're being truthful and consistent in your responses to the various questions. Let's go over the actual profile . . . the scores above the top line are suggestive of problem areas or conflicts . . . the four scale, uh, see the numbers for each scale . . .

Mary: Yes . . . It looks like the number four is the highest, but the two, and seven, and uh . . . nine are above that dark line too.

Doctor F: That's right, but let's focus on the four scale first, and then we'll get to some of the symptoms or difficulties that usually go with the other scales later, okay? Elevations such as yours on the four scale are often related to problems with being impulsive, taking risks, and alcohol or drug abuse as well as acting-out . . . or doing things without thinking of the consequences . . . the nine scale with the four scale can indicate problems with authority, or legal difficulties too, and self-centeredness . . . uh, plus manipulation or anger issues . . . the two is depression . . . and your score of sixty-eight suggests mild depression . . . like low self-esteem, low energy, or feeling tired a lot, and probably feeling down on yourself or sad . . . maybe sleep problems?

Mary: That test is right on, Doc . . . so far . . . I've sure had a lot of problems with the law, and I've got a short fuse too . . . people do piss me off! I guess the DUI arrests, and all the men . . . I mean my husbands and the poor choices could be part of it too . . . ha, ha . . . I've always had problems with men, and drugs, and sex! I never worry about the consequences, and that's probably why I get into so much trouble . . . It's the same old shit!

Doctor F: Anxiety or feeling stressed and also being kind of compulsive or even perfectionistic can also go with your seven scale elevation, Mary . . . Do those traits or characteristics seem to fit you?

Mary: The stress and anxiety really fits . . . and I'm still really nervous about my last DUI. That's number three, and my lawyer told me I could go to jail for maybe a year . . . My blood alcohol level was real high, and I got one a year ago . . . I'm real nervous about it too, Doc, and that's why my lawyer wanted me to come in for this evaluation . . . I hope you can help keep me out of jail; I'm sure nervous about going to jail!

Doctor F: It seems to fit . . . the anxiety piece . . . and the fear, or being nervous about going to jail.

Mary: You got that one right, Doc, but why do I keep doing this shit? I mean I was really drunk; my BAC was a .24 . . . it seems like I never learn . . . ha . . . ha . . . That compulsive thing you mentioned a bit a go might be right on, too . . . Maybe I'm a compulsive "drunk driver?" At least, I haven't had any accidents. And I'm pissed about paying those damned lawyers and fines and stuff . . . and you're not cheap either.

Doctor F: Well, I can sense that you're being honest and open with me about your test results . . . and it sounds like they do describe some or maybe a lot of your behaviors pretty accurately. Most people with alcoholism or severe drinking problems find it difficult to stop, or stay stopped . . . it is a compulsive and impulsive thing, and engaging in the same destructive patterns of behavior over and over can also be a part of it too. Trying to be honest with me . . . and being honest and open in your responses to the test will help "us" better figure out what's really going on with you, and hopefully . . . to help you change . . . plus openness and honesty . . . and "commitment" to treatment on your part will help you change, and get on with your life . . . instead of continuing to do the same old destructive stuff, over and over . . . Does this make any sense to you?

Mary: Yeah, but I've never been consistent at anything, except drinking and getting in trouble . . . at least it seems that way.

This vignette again demonstrates the relevance and importance of therapist or clinician and patient self-disclosure in assessing and diagnosing substance use disorders. The author openly and honestly explained the various emotional and behavioral difficulties that were associated with Mary's MMPI-II test results, and Mary also seemed to honestly self-disclose about the congruence between her test results and some of the significant persistent difficulties she had experienced in her life.

This brief therapy vignette also demonstrates how diagnostic testing and clinical assessment are very important transitional components in the process of intensive psychotherapy and treatment for many chemically dependent persons. The client's responses to the therapist's exploration of test results provided further diagnostic and treatment data pertaining to her motivation and readiness for therapy, insight and awareness, capacity for change, and other therapeutic relational dynamics. Working and productive therapeutic alliances are often formed during the diagnostic and clinical assessment stages of the treatment process.

THERAPIST AND CLIENT SELF-DISCLOSURE IN THE CHEMICAL DEPENDENCY COUNSELING RELATIONSHIP

Effective counseling and psychotherapy relationships involving a diversity of patient populations in large measure develop vis-à-vis the counselor's ability to consistently provide high-level therapeutic conditions within the context of the therapeutic relationship (Forrest, 1994, 1997, 2009; Hill and Lent, 2006; Kirschenbaum and Jourdan, 2005; Klein, et al, 2001; Rogers, 1957, 1961; Truax and Carkhuff, 1967). Therapist high-level facilitative conditions include nonpossessive warmth, empathy, genuineness, and concreteness (Forrest, 1992, 1994, 1997; Kirschenbaum and Jourdan, 2005; Norcross, Bike and Evans, 2009; Rogers, 1957; Truax and Carkhuff, 1967). These facilitative therapist conditions or core ingredients in effective counseling relationships (Forrest, 1992, 1994, 2002, 2009) also pertain to the treatment relationship with chemically dependent and substance-abusing persons.

Counselor genuineness and authenticity always involves and evolves via the counselor's capacity for healthy and appropriate self-disclosing behavior. As indicated earlier in this chapter, counselor genuineness and authenticity or self-disclosure are important ingredients in the diagnostic and ongoing assessment process in psychotherapy relationships with chemically dependent clients. Counselor genuineness and self-disclosing behaviors are also key ingredients in every facet of the initial and later stages of intensive individual psychotherapy involving chemically dependent and substance-abusing persons.

During the initial stage of intensive psychotherapy or counseling, the chemical dependency counselor begins to work with the client to establish a working and productive therapeutic alliance. This process begins with a diagnostic assessment of the client, continues during the initial counseling sessions as the counselor and client develop a structured treatment and recovery plan, and then continues throughout the various stages of the psychotherapeutic process (Forrest, 1997, 2002, 2007, 2009). Counselor or therapist self-disclosures constitute an important ingredient in the communications and ongoing therapeutic interactions, which convey an emotional climate or therapeutic atmosphere that is characterized by high levels of counselor nonpossessive warmth, empathy, genuineness, and concreteness. These counselor ingredients are central to the establishment and maintenance of an ongoing, productive, and working therapeutic alliance with chemically dependent and substance-abusing clients (Forrest, 1992, 1994, 1997, 2006, 2007, 2009).

The structural components of effective counseling and therapy relationships with chemically dependent persons (Forrest, 1994, 1997, 2008) involve (1) the therapeutic relationship or alliance, (2) self-help involvement (Alcoholics Anonymous, Cocaine Anonymous, etc. with active sponsorship) and/or support group/group therapy involvement, (3) an active, consistent, and medically appropriate ongoing exercise regimen, (4) a recovery-based nutritional program, (5) possible psychotropic or other appropriate medications and ongoing or time limited medication management, (6) spouse, significant other, and/or family treatment and self-help care, (7) possible detoxification, medical care, residential and/or IOP (Intensive Out-Patient) treatment,

(8) spiritual and/or possible church-based religious activities, and (9) other individually-based and cognitive-behavior oriented interventions such as assertion training, anger management, relaxation training, divorce recovery, self-esteem enhancement, and relationship skills training. The counselor or therapist actively works with the chemically dependent or substance-abusing client to facilitate the client's participation and ongoing engagement in a structured treatment regimen that is based upon the particular treatment needs of each client. Counselor and client openness, genuineness, and ongoing self-disclosures are essential to the process of helping the client and counselors develop a commitment to an appropriate, individualized, and efficacious structured treatment plan.

Within the explicit context of the therapeutic alliance, effective counselors continually express and communicate empathy, genuineness, nonpossessive warmth and concreteness vis-à-vis their ongoing verbal interactions, self-disclosures, and dynamic cognitive-behavioral as well as effective interacting with clients. Working and productive therapeutic alliances evolve as a process and require both counselor and client commitment to the ongoing development of a relationship that is a potent and meaningful vehicle for change. Mutual trust, respect, and concern are also essential ingredients of the therapeutic alliance. The basic humanness and interpersonal relatedness of the therapeutic alliance is curative.

The counselor or therapist is a "real person" within the therapeutic encounter. Working and productive alliances involve strategic counselor interpretations, feedback and confrontations, didactic and experiential teaching, education, and self disclosures. Therapists can actively teach substance-abusing persons to practice honest self-disclosing behavior.

As indicated earlier by the author (Forrest, 1994, 1997, 2002, 2009), the initial stage of counseling and intensive individual therapeutic work with alcoholics and substance abusers encompasses the first two to four months of weekly or every other week counseling sessions. While brief therapy and managed care companies have generally shortened and limited therapeutic care over the past ten years, dynamically-oriented counselors and therapist that often provide therapy for self-paying clients (Forrest, 2008, 2009), who also tend to be more internally motivated to enter and sustain ongoing treatment relationships, continue to see chemically dependent or substance-abusing persons on a weekly or regular basis for several months or even years. These counselors and therapists can focus on (1) developing a working and productive therapeutic alliance, (2) initiating and sustaining genetic reconstruction work, (3) initiating and sustaining an addiction or chemical dependency/therapy focus, and (4) supportively and consistently confronting (Forrest 1992) clients about the various dynamics and parameters of their chemical dependency or substance abuse during the initial stage of counseling.

It is also of paramount importance for the counselor or therapist to emphasize the importance of the client's commitment to initiating and sustaining drug abstinence during this stage of treatment. The counselor correspondingly discloses and communicates to the client his or her ongoing commitment to the therapeutic task or goal of helping the client to achieve their *mutual* therapeutic goals. Motivational interviewing (Dunn, Neighbors and Larimer, 2006; Miller and Rollinick, 2002; Packard, 2009) can also be very therapeutic at this juncture in the therapeutic process.

Counselor and client discourse in each of these realms is rife with self-disclosure. However, the specific genetic reconstruction work of this stage of counseling or therapy is much more focused upon the client's disclosures pertaining to childhood, adolescence, and life-long sources of profound narcissistic injury and trauma (Forrest, 1985, 1994, 1997, 2008). Counselors and therapists need to supportively and consistently explain and disclose to the client the relevance and therapeutic value of this facet of therapeutic intervention during the initial weeks and months of therapy with these clients. However, the process of genetic reconstruction work (Forrest, 1997) is clearly constructed around the self-disclosures of the client and the therapist's active efforts to foster client openness and self-disclosing behaviors.

Developing and maintaining an addiction focus during the initial as well as subsequent stages of intensive psychotherapy with substance abusers and chemically dependent clients (Forrest, 1997, 2006, 2009) constitutes a core therapeutic task that is essential to successful work with these individuals. The client is consistently encouraged to disclose his or her current and historic thoughts, beliefs, experiences, attitude, feelings, and relational dynamics associated with life experiences as well as mood-altering drugs. The counselor also provides feedback, support, clarification, interpretations, education, and employs myriad cognitive-behavioral interventions to help the client adaptively modify various beliefs, thoughts, behaviors, relationships, and emotions that have helped develop and sustain his or her maladaptive addictive behaviors and global adjustment style. Ongoing counselor and client self-disclosures are essential to the process of maintaining an addiction focus in therapy. This therapeutic process also helps to elucidate and modify or extinguish the various "triggers" and factors that have historically maintained and reinforced the client's substance abuse and relapse history. Thus, very early in the therapeutic relationship these intervention strategies become deterrents to relapse and constitute a relational form of relapse prevention.

Effective confrontation strategies (Forrest, 1992) need to be supportive and are also based upon a working and productive therapeutic alliance involving high levels of therapist nonpossessive warmth, empathy, genuineness, and concreteness. Counselors frequently self-disclose vis-à-vis their confrontation-based interactions with the client early and throughout the course of therapeutic work with substance abusers and chemically dependent clients. Therapeutic confrontation occurs when the counselor provides the client with diagnostic and assessment results. Various forms and levels of therapeutic confrontation take place whenever the counselor provides feedback to the client. Counselor self-disclosures and confrontation occur whenever the counselor openly shares his or her feedback, perceptions and observations, beliefs, thoughts and feelings about the client, himself, or the counseling relationship with the client. All of these transactions involving feedback from the counselor to the client or from the client to counselor involve mutual self-disclosure as well as some level of mutual confrontation.

Counselor and client self-disclosures are also germane to the counselor's continual examination and exploration of the client's involvement and commitment to the basic structural components of treatment and recovery throughout the therapeutic process.

The middle stage of intensive therapeutic work with this clinical population (Forrest, 1997, 2009) generally takes place between the third or fourth month and sixth to eighth month of individual therapy. The essential therapist intervention strategies during this stage of treatment (Forrest, 1999. 2009) involve more active interpretations and promoting client insight and self-awareness, managing and dealing with resistance, transference and countertransference, implementing a more here-and-now based therapeutic focus, utilizing various cognitive-behavioral modalities, providing sex counseling and education or sex therapy interventions when indicated, and the continued use of confrontation and relapse prevention techniques. Counselor or therapist and client self-disclosures are once again at the heart of each of these essential middle stage therapist intervention strategies. Counselors and therapists continually self-disclose about various facets of their being vis-à-vis their interpretations, style of dealing with such issues as transference and countertransference, and implementation of cognitive-behavioral counseling interventions, sex education or therapy, relapse prevention, and confrontation.

Much of the affect-focused work of the middle stage of intensive chemical dependency counseling also evolves from the intensified reciprocal self-disclosures between the counselor and client. As counselors and therapists attempt to clarify, examine and explore, understand, and foster "corrective emotional experiences" (Alexander, 1956) upon the part of their clients, their personal affective, cognitive, and behavioral self-disclosures impact the affective realm of the therapeutic relationship. Affectively charged client and counselor self-disclosures may, in fact, significantly impact and change virtually any facet of the client-counselor or therapeutic relationship. And this change (Forrest 1984) can always be for better or worse.

The later stages of counseling and intensive therapeutic work with substance abusers and chemically dependent persons (Forrest, 1997, 2006, 2009) involves ongoing counselor self-disclosures associated with synthesis and working through, helping the recovering client continue the process of identity consolidation, resolving projective identification issues, more intensive affective work, and termination. Counselors and therapists who utilize dream work, relapse prevention training, and after-care interventions during this juncture in the therapeutic process also employ various levels of self-disclosing behavior with their clients. Obviously, clients also continue to self-disclose in response to these treatment strategies, the therapeutic alliance, and a diversity of other issues later in therapy.

During the later stages of the psychotherapeutic process, counselor and client self-disclosures may be more in-depth, affective, and direct. The strength and depth of the therapeutic alliance fosters increased mutual self-disclosure, and a strong therapeutic alliance also builds mutual trust between the client and therapist. A working and productive therapeutic alliance becomes a vehicle for containing, resolving and working through, and neutralizing powerful emotions and affects as well as other potential sources of both constructive growth and change and destructive conflicts or regression associated with the more in-depth self-disclosures of the therapist and client. The intense, in-depth, and sometimes brutally honest self-disclosures of the counselor or client associated with these later stages of therapy may have resulted in premature treatment termination or a serious rupture in the therapeutic alliance during the middle or early stages of therapy.

The termination phase of intensive therapeutic work with chemically dependent persons (Forrest, 1997, 2009) involves a good deal of mutual ongoing self-disclosing behavior between the therapist and client. This stage of therapy involves consistent feedback and re-processing of prior treatment based material between client and therapist as well as a here-and-now focus on the various feelings and dynamics associated with actual treatment termination. The effective therapeutic management of these issues can only occur via the self-disclosures, open exploration, and therapeutic focus of both the counselor and client.

The following case studies demonstrate the importance of client and counselor self-disclosure at different points or stages in the psychotherapeutic process:

Case 2: Jerry C. was a thirty-year-old executive. He was referred to the author by his attorney following a recent third arrest for DUI. The client had a BAC of .16 at the time of the arrest and was unable to recall the BAC level for his first DUI. His second DUI arrest occurred three years earlier. Mr. C. openly acknowledged his culpability in these arrests and stressed the nature of his "poor decision making" during his initial three therapy sessions. The client was a bright, successful, and articulate young man who felt very strongly that he did *not* manifest alcoholism or a severe alcohol abuse problem. He acknowledged that he did "binge drink" one or two times each week while playing poker with his colleagues or "bar-hopping" with friends.

Mr. C. failed to show up for his fourth therapy session and then called for another appointment two weeks later. The client reported in this session that he had again been arrested for DUI (BAC .132) and presented with an extremely despondent and depressive manner. Mr. C. spent most of this session focusing upon the cost of his DUI arrests, and he had considerable anxiety about his job situation as well as worries about not being able to drive to and from work. His drivers license had been confiscated by the arresting officer. The client was seen three weeks later after he had attended a court hearing with his attorney. During this session, the client's general demeanor was rather dramatically changed. Mr. C. disclosed that he had consciously minimized and lied to the author about his drinking behavior and a number of other issues during his initial therapy sessions, and he also indicated that he had been "reflecting" about many issues associated with his life and lifestyle over the past few weeks. Most of his friendships and social relationships were built around heavy drinking and "partying." The client disclosed that he had always felt insecure, was preoccupied about his weight and appearance, and his childhood and adolescence were extremely conflicted.

Mr. C's radical shift to openness, honesty, and a more self-disclosing style at this juncture in the therapy process also impacted the author's therapeutic stance. I responded to the client's disclosures by disclosing that I had initially sensed that he was minimizing and denying the severity of his drinking disorder and also related this disclosure to his elevated k-sub-scale and general results of his MMPI-II test results. Within the context of this therapy session and the following session, our therapeutic relationship changed in a very significant and positive manner. The client's third DUI arrest and his subsequent emotional and cognitive changes coupled with our mutually more open, honest, and self-disclosing dialogue provided the foundation for developing a working and productive therapeutic alliance.

The client was subsequently seen within the context of every other week psychotherapy for seven months and then on a monthly or every other month basis for eight months. He successfully completed a number of state-mandated alcohol/drug education and treatment requirements and spent some three months in a community connections program. Mr. C. has remained totally alcohol abstinent for over three and one-half years and also continues to be involved in a weekly education and recovery support group. Unlike many chemically dependent or substance abusing client's, Mr. C.'s legal crisis shortly after engaging in therapy facilitated his capacity to initiate more open, honest, and self-disclosing transactions in therapy, which also fostered the author's self-disclosing feedback, the establishment of a working therapeutic alliance, and a successful treatment outcome.

The interactive, relational, and curative synergy of therapist and client self-disclosure is central to this case study. This case study demonstrates how crisis situations during the early stage of counseling and intensive psychotherapy can precipitate levels of both client and counselor self-disclosing behaviors, which can greatly enhance and quicken the development of a working and productive therapeutic alliance.

Case three demonstrates the potential impact of therapist and client self-disclosures during the middle stages of counseling and intensive therapeutic work with chemically dependent and substance-abusing persons.

Case 3: Julie M. was a forty-four-year-old married professional woman. The client was initially seen within the context of conjoint marital therapy. Her husband of nearly twenty years initiated therapy and had given Julie an ultimatum to "get into treatment, or we get divorced." The M's were seen within the context of three conjoint marital sessions, and then Julie began individual psychotherapy. The client was very defensive about her drinking behavior during these initial conjoint sessions, but did acknowledge she had a "drinking problem." She also verbalized that she had "other problems." A consensus of opinion was reached between both clients and the author that individual therapy was indicated for Julie.

Julie was subsequently seen within the context of individual psychotherapy on a weekly or every other week basis for eight months. Early in therapy, Julie established a pattern of remaining alcohol abstinent for a few days of perhaps two weeks at a time, and then she would "binge drink" for one to three days. During the early stage of therapy, she disclosed to the author that she had been consuming between one pint and one quart of vodka on a daily basis for over five years. Her husband had no awareness about the extent of her drinking problem; however, she had experienced alcohol related work difficulties. The M's had no children and her extended family was aware of her alcohol dependence. The client also disclosed that she would frequently (two to three times per week) consume a pint of vodka before completing a one-hour high intensity aerobics class noting that virtually "no one" could detect when she was drinking . . . even when she was "really drunk."

After three or four months of consistent therapeutic involvement and very sporadic Alcoholics Anonymous participation, the client came to an afternoon appointment late. The author suspected that she had been drinking but she was, in fact, very articulate and certainly did not smell like alcohol or manifest other symptoms of intoxication or alcohol induced behavioral impairment. I directly and assertively disclosed my suspicion and concerns about her drinking, and she vehemently denied having consumed alcohol prior to our session! I then disclosed that she was never late for therapy sessions and not only was this a first, but her facial complexion and particularly her nose, were as *red* as wine. Her facial complexion had always been white and certainly without *any* redness. After several minutes of this discussion, Mrs. M. acknowledged that she had consumed "one or two drinks" with her lunch prior to our therapy session.

Mrs. M. stated that she had only consumed "two drinks at most" with lunch and then acknowledged that her face had "always" turned red following drinking, but that this occurred naturally at her high intensity aerobics classes and most of the other participants also became red-faced with rigorous exercise. Thus, others in the class could not discover that she was drinking by the color of her skin and nose. However, she also disclosed that her husband had learned that her red face and nose meant she had been drinking and more often than not meant that she was drunk.

At the end of our session, I told the client that she would need to call her husband, someone else, or perhaps a cab to pick her up. I explained to her that I could not allow her to leave my office and drive knowing that she had been drinking. Following a discussion of the ethics and liability of this situation, Mrs. M. agreed to walk across the street with me to a community hospital and complete a breathalyzer test to "prove" that she was not "legally intoxicated." She assured the author that she was sober and her BAC level would be well below the .05 level required in Colorado for a "driving while ability impaired" arrest and legal conviction. To the disbelief of Mrs. M. and *myself,* her BAC level was .187! We left the hospital emergency room, returned to my office, and I called her husband to come and pick up his wife. After briefly explaining these events to Mr. M., I scheduled the patient to be seen the following week.

The following week Mrs. M. arrived for her therapy session early and sober. She reported she had been attending AA meetings each day and had also gotten a "temporary sponsor" since our last meeting. The client also verbalized that she was still in disbelief about her BAC level, but she openly acknowledged that she had lied to me about the amount of alcohol she had consumed prior to our session. She apologized about putting me at some legal risk in this matter and then disclosed that she had repeatedly wondered about my facial complexion and even ruminated about the possibility of my drinking prior to therapy sessions because of the color of my nose and face! I assured the client that I did not drink or ingest other mood-altering drugs prior to our therapy sessions and disclosed at some length to the client about my acne, extremely fair complexion, former carrot red hair (I have essentially been bald for nearly twenty years) and chronic skin condition. We both laughed about these matters, and I also self-disclosed some information about my personal alcohol abuse some forty years earlier when I was an undergraduate student and fraternity member.

Julie continued in individual psychotherapy for some four months and was then seen infrequently as a part of the termination and follow-up stages of treatment. She has remained totally alcohol abstinent for over four years, and she continues to attend Alcoholics Anonymous two to three times per week and is involved in a women's recovery support group. The client's self-disclosures and increased openness associated with continued relapses during the middle stage of therapy played an important role in her recovery. The author's personal disclosures that were related to Mrs. M's bodily disclosure or betrayal of her continued drinking and denial also seemed to improve the depth and strength of the therapeutic alliance.

The client later disclosed to the author that her sponsor and others in the AA community had hold her that most therapists and doctors are not able to understand or help alcoholics and most other addicts because of their personal problems or because they are not recovering addicts. By disclosing about some of my drinking experiences that took place many years earlier and by openly disclosing about my chronic skin condition, Mrs. M. further disclosed that she became more aware of my humanness, frailty, and vulnerabilities while at the same time developing a deeper sense of respect for me and my commitment to help her change. These realities also seemed to reinforce and strengthen her commitment to treatment, abstinence, recovery, and the change process.

Therapist and client self-disclosures are essential to effective therapeutic work at every juncture in the therapeutic process. However, the depth, scope, and affective parameters of therapist and client self-disclosures may be relatively or radically different at different points in therapy. Therapists generally tend to be more open and disclosing during the middle and later stages of intensive psychotherapeutic work with chemically dependent persons (Forrest, 2002, 2005, 2008) as well as other patient or client populations (Glasser, 2000, 2003, 2005). Client and therapist self-disclosing behavior can also be central to the therapeutic relationship during the process of treatment termination and even after termination of a formal therapeutic relationship.

The following therapy vignette demonstrates the nature of constructive therapist and client self-disclosures that can occur after an extended formal therapeutic relationship has been successfully terminated.

Doctor F: It's really good to see you, Julie . . . It's been a long time since you've been in; how are things going?

Julie M.: Well, I'm doing okay . . . really pretty good . . . I mean, I'm still sober, but I've been thinking about some of the things we talked about a couple of years ago when we were only meeting every two or three months, and I remember what you said about making an appointment in the future if I needed to, and really . . . I've needed to for two or three months.

Doctor F: So what's happening? I'm glad you called and made an appointment! What took so long? Ha, Ha.

Julie M.: It's been a year since I saw you last, and I've been doing fine . . . it's been easy to stay sober, and I still go to a few meetings every week, but Bob and I are still having problems, and I met a guy in the program three of four months ago, and I . . . uh, well I've gotten emotionally involved with him . . . uh, no sex yet, but it's scary . . . Bob and I have been together for over eight years . . . and, uh, I mean it's really not that bad with Bob.

Doctor F: I guess Bob doesn't know about the other guy, or does he suspect?

Julie M.: Hell no, he doesn't have clue . . . but I'm always on his case and he has been asking me what's wrong and forever on me about not working my program . . . and he's right about it, I've started to obsess and fantasize about Jack for a month or two . . . and he's married too, and has three kids.

Doctor F: So the good news is that you've decided to get back into therapy, called me . . . and you've also mentioned that it's only emotional at this point . . . not sexual?

Julie M.: That's right, Doctor Gary, but we're both struggling. . . . You probably remember that Bob and I never really had much of a sex life together . . . once every couple of months and it was over in two seconds, plus like I told you, he had a "whiskey-dick" for the first two years or so that we got together . . . and Jack says his wife isn't really interested in sex either . . . I guess it's a mess, but I don't want it to get worse . . . I need to think this thing through and I need some help . . . that's why I'm here, and I even feel better now just starting to tell you about what's happening.

Doctor F: Have you discussed any of this with your sponsor, or have you been trying to work it out on your own over the past couple of months?

Julie M.: I didn't want to talk to my sponsor about it. I felt kinda embarrassed and ashamed . . . plus even though she has over fifteen years in the program, I know her relationship with her husband leaves a lot to be desired . . . but I did tell her about our lack of sex in the marriage a few days ago. She knows Bob has a lot of problems, and she did suggest that both of us should talk to you . . . she actually told me that maybe I needed to get back to therapy with or without Bob.

Doctor F: Sounds like you've got a good sponsor, Julie . . . plus you listened to her and took some action to deal with the situation. . . . Do you remember us talking about relapse, trying to prevent relapses, and "triggers" a couple of years ago . . . recognizing your relapse triggers and sources of conflict related to relapse and seeking help before a relapse . . . like heading it off or dealing with other problems before they mushroom . . . I remember us talking about *me* and not wanting to deal with that lump on my gum . . . talk about fear and some denial . . . ha . . .

Julie M: I remember all of that like it was yesterday . . . it makes me realize again that none of us are perfect, not even you . . . ha, ha . . . but I'm sure glad you reminded me of that . . . and thinking back about it, we talked a lot about my marital situation and sex in therapy. . . . You also warned me or tried to get me to deal with it then, but I guess I wasn't ready or maybe I just thought the problem would go away if I stayed sober long enough . . . I sure thought Bob would get over that "whiskey dick" thing . . . low desire is what you called it but he's never really been romantic or intimate with me either . . . and he's been sober for years but he never wanted to deal with it in therapy. . . . Remember, he told me a number of times that therapy wasn't helping me and that it was a waste of time and money.

Doctor F: I do remember most of that, Julie, and I also remember that you separated from Bob after two or three months of therapy. When you were first getting sober and feeling better about yourself . . . and less depressed.

Julie M.: Listening to you helps . . . deep down I know I need to deal with my relationship with Bob before I even consider having sex with Jack or really getting involved with him. . . . I'm not sure I can do it, but maybe I need to tell him now that we need to end it . . . the relationship. Deep down, I know I really don't want, or need, to be involved with Jack . . . maybe it's basically a sex thing?

Doctor F: Julie, my honest and direct feedback to you at this point is just don't get involved with Jack . . . we need to get back on track with a few booster sessions or maybe ongoing therapy for a few months and try to resolve these issues.

This follow-up therapy vignette with Julie M. illustrates the clinical importance and therapeutic parameters of continued client and therapist self-disclosure during and actually following therapy termination. Julie had been seen in three or four termination focused (Forrest, 1997) therapy sessions over the course of a year, completed therapy, and then several months later she re-engaged in treatment following the development of a budding extramarital relationship. The client was very ambivalent and conflicted in her marital relationship as well as conflicted about becoming involved in an affair. She disclosed these various issues with the author, and I also openly disclosed my sentiments pertaining to her situation. She re-engaged in active therapy and was seen within the context of eight subsequent sessions. Julie terminated her evolving relationship with Jack, and she and her husband entered conjoint marital therapy with another therapist. She is sober and has continued to remain married. However, her marital relationship remains significantly conflicted.

IATROGENIC SELF-DISCLOSURE IN CHEMICAL DEPENDENCY COUNSELING RELATIONSHIPS

Therapist and client self-disclosures in chemical dependency counseling (Forrest, 1999, 2002, 2008) can always have a "for better or worse" impact upon the counselor, client, and the therapeutic relationship. Counselor or therapist self-disclosures can have an adverse impact on the client, therapeutic alliance, or even the counselor. Client transparency and self-disclosures also can adversely impact the therapist, therapeutic alliance, or the client.

As noted throughout this text, it is impossible to predict the precise impact or effect of counselor and client self-disclosures in therapy. Furthermore, the immediate or short-term impact of a disclosure may be very different than the extended or long-term effect of a disclosure. This reality applies equally to counselors, clients, and their therapeutic relationships. These factors have been consistently related to the ongoing need for "therapist" foresight, sensitivity, and reasoned judgment when using self-disclosure based interventions with chemically dependent persons and other clients (Bridges, 2001; Farber, Khurgin-Bott and Feldman, 2009; Forrest, 2002, 2006, Hill and Lenox, 2001; Myers and Hayes, 2006; Peterson, 2002; Roes, 2004). The research and clinical effects of counselor or therapist self-disclosures on clients and to a lesser extent, the therapeutic relationship, were also examined earlier in this book. Clearly, this data also reinforces the importance of good general therapist acumen when disclosing to clients in counseling and therapy relationships.

To the contrary, there are virtually no current or historic research data available that address the impact of client self-disclosures upon specific therapist behaviors or the temporal behavior and psychological functioning of counselors and therapists. As discussed earlier in the book, limited research evidence (Truax and Carkhuff, 1967) does indicate that high levels of client self-disclosure early in therapy relate to more favorable treatment outcomes. However, thousands of clinically oriented articles and text books have anecdotally reported upon the general effects of patient self-disclosures upon therapists, patients, and the therapeutic relationship (Forrest, 1994, 2002, Fromm-Reichman, 1949; Glasser, 2000, 2005, Reik, 1948; Sullivan, 1953).

As discussed earlier in this chapter, client self-disclosure and openness is especially important early in the therapeutic or counseling relationship. Client self-disclosures are essential to accurately assessing and diagnosing chemically dependent clients and then providing appropriate treatment interventions during the early stage of therapy. The client's initial self-disclosures may or may not result in a clinician's decision to hospitalize, refer for medication, refer for detoxification, recommend residential or intensive outpatient therapy, and so forth. Honest, forthright, grossly dishonest, or a lack of client self-disclosures, may impact every facet of the early as well as later stages of the treatment process. The client's inability to disclose and honestly explore a plethora of issues with the therapist at any juncture in the therapeutic relationship may prove tantamount to treatment failure or even contribute to the client's death. Severe iatrogenic treatment effects can be associated with a lack of client openness, self-disclosure, and basic honesty with the therapist during initial diagnostic and therapeutic sessions as well as during subsequent stages of therapy.

Clients who are unable to consistently and honestly disclose to the counselor during the initial stage of intensive psychotherapy may prematurely terminate therapy, repeatedly relapse, or prove to be generally more treatment resistant. However, many clients who are nondisclosing and resistive early in therapy will develop the capacity for more open and honest disclosing behavior if they are able to establish initial alcohol/drug abstinence, sustain their involvement in therapy, and are working with a counselor or therapist who is able to provide consistently high level therapeutic conditions in the therapeutic relationship (Forrest, 1997, 2008).

Effective chemical dependency counselors actively encourage and reinforce client self-disclosing behavior early and throughout the process of effective psychotherapy relationships. Most substance-abusing clients become progressively more open, honest, and disclosing within the therapeutic relationship if they persist in therapy, develop a more trusting relationship with the therapist, and as the therapeutic alliance is strengthened. Alcohol and drug abstinence is central to this process as is the therapist's continued reinforcement of client openness, transparency, and rigorous honesty. All of these factors contribute significantly to an enhanced depth of the therapeutic relationship, which becomes curative and reparative for many chemically dependent clients. In effect, effective therapists teach their chemically dependent clients healthy self-disclosing behaviors in myriad ways.

More open and self-disclosing client behaviors occur rather spontaneously during the middle and later stages of therapy with substance abusers and chemically dependent clients. The client's increased capacity for in-depth self-disclosure and genuineness later in the therapeutic relationship contributes to the ongoing process of constructive personality growth and change.

The client's self-disclosures can also have a psychonoxious or iatrogenic effect upon the client, therapist, or therapeutic relationship at virtually any juncture in the treatment process. Clients who have repressed, minimized, and denied a plethora of early-childhood as well as life-long narcissistic injuries (Forrest, 1999) and trauma are especially prone to re-traumatizing the self during the early stages of therapy vis-à-vis their self-disclosures to the counselor. While this aspect of the client's therapeutic behavior is cathartic and essential to many other facets of the change process, it is nonetheless very painful, difficult, and anxiety-provoking for most primary alcoholics and chemically dependent persons. In part, the client's self-disclosures early in therapy can be painful and self-traumatizing as a function of alcohol and/or drug abstinence. The newly-drug abstinent client usually feels anxious, vulnerable, internally threatened, and conflicted by a diversity of emotions, cognitions, and past behaviors that he or she must begin to cope with in the absence of drug intoxication. These various realities can be essential triggers or precursors to relapse early in therapy (Forrest, 1985, 1994, 1997, 2009). However, the client's active engagement and commitment to a structured and intensive program of recovery at this point usually proves to be a strong deterrent to relapse. Drug abstinence, detoxification, and possibly drug withdrawal are also traumatic factors that contribute to the patients anxiety and vulnerability to relapse at this juncture (early stage) of the treatment and recovery process.

Chemically dependent persons who sustain their involvements in intensive psychotherapy and an ongoing structured recovery program progressively resolve, modify, and neutralize these sources of early and middle stage recovery facilitated conflicts through their continued self-disclosures and enhanced capacity for openness, honesty, and authenticity with their counselors, sponsors, and significant others in recovery. The client's various historic as well as current sources of trauma, narcissistic injury, and conflict can only be resolved and changed through the ongoing mediums of human interaction, communication, and honest self-disclosing behaviors.

Counselors and therapists can also potentially facilitate emotional distress and anxiety in their clients as a result of their self-disclosures in therapy. Therapist induced anxiety and transference reactions (Forrest, 1994, 1997, 2002, 2007) in clients can always be helpful or potentially harmful to the client and the treatment relationship.

Iatrogenic or psychonoxious therapist self-disclosures often stem from premature interpretations, direct and non-empathic confrontations, untimely and intensive affective work, poor management of client resistance, relapse and acting-out in therapy, and general transference as well as countertransference dynamics. Therapists also may disclose personal life experiences and information to clients that can be anxiety provoking or in other ways potentially upsetting. It is important to emphasize that the counselor's self-disclosures may adversely impact one client, therapeutically help another client, and perhaps have little, if any, impact on others. It is always difficult, if not impossible, for therapists and counselors to be able to strategically predict the precise impact of a given self-disclosure upon a particular client or group of clients. However, a relatively small subset of therapists (Forrest, 1994, 2009; Norcross, 2002; Truax and Carkhuff, 1967) seem to consistently impact their clients in a psychonoxious manner, which results in generally poor treatment outcomes. The self-disclosing demeanor or style of these therapists may be partially responsible for their consistently poor treatment outcomes.

The following case study shows how therapist self-disclosures can adversely affect the client as well as the therapeutic relationship.

Case 4: Susan M. was referred to the author for individual therapy by another psychologist, who had been treating Susan's adolescent son. Mrs. M's adolescent son had repeatedly told his therapist that he was "very upset" about his mother's drinking behavior and the therapist discussed this with Susan. Susan acknowledged that she "knew" she has drinking "too much" and agreed to enter therapy with the author. The client was a forty-three-year-old housewife who had been previously married to three other men. These prior marital relationships had all ended in divorce within six months; however, she had been married to her current husband for seventeen years and they had one fifteen year old son. Mrs. M. was a homemaker, but she had sustained a professional career a number of years earlier as a real-estate broker. Her husband was a very wealthy and successful businessman who had been "out of town on business, three weeks out of four" for the duration of the marriage.

After completing an initial intake and history-focused initial therapy session with Susan, the author saw the client in four subsequent individual therapy sessions over the course of some six weeks. Susan also completed an MMPI-II after her second therapy session, and we developed a structured recovery and treatment plan together. The client was initially open about her drinking history and acknowledged that she had been consuming between "six and ten" glasses of wine each night for "over twenty years, since I went to college." She also reported that her biological father died from chronic alcoholism at forty-eight years of age (cirrhosis) and her biological mother was actively alcoholic at age sixty-seven. Furthermore, several of her extended family members had also experienced severe drinking problems including a maternal aunt who had been killed in a drunk-driving accident several years earlier. Mrs. M. was aware of her son's concerns about her drinking, and she also indicated that her husband had voiced his concerns about her drinking on many occasions over the past year or two.

I continued to supportively encourage Mrs. M. to begin attending a women's open AA meeting each week and/or my weekly education and recovery support group, complete a medical exam with blood work and liver enzyme studies, begin some form of medically appropriate exercise regimen, and actively engage in other adjunctive treatment interventions that we had discussed in our initial two or three sessions. It became increasingly apparent that Mrs. M. was ambivalent about being in therapy and terminating her alcohol dependence. She openly stated that she was worried about who might see here at self-help meetings or my group. She was also understandably anxious about seeing her physician and possibly being labeled an "alcoholic." During our fourth session, Mrs. M. reported that she felt very positive about "cutting back" her nightly wine consumption to "six, or at most, eight" glasses of wine each night but she also noted that she felt "shaky" in the mornings and at time experienced difficulties with her sense of balance.

I spent a good deal of our fourth session encouraging and trying to supportively motivate the client to see her physician as soon as possible and openly discussing the potential risks associated with alcohol withdrawal. We also explored the treatment options of residential care and a possible brief hospitalization or inpatient detoxification. I was very open and self-disclosing about the potential risks as well as helpful and preventative aspects associated with these treatment alternatives. We discussed these issues in some depth, the client processed my input, asked questions, and verbalized that she did not feel that her drinking was that "out of control." She wanted to continue in therapy with me, felt I would help her become abstinent, and scheduled another appointment. Prior to terminating our fourth session, I again openly disclosed my concerns, experiences, and honest impression about her need for medical care specific to stopping drinking.

The client did not show up for her scheduled appointment the following week. My secretary called and encouraged the client to re-schedule, but she indicated that she was doing "great," her earlier sessions with me had been very helpful, and she would call to reschedule again if she experienced further difficulties. Eleven months later Mrs. M. was seen for consultation following a DUI arrest. Her BAC level at the time of the arrest was .260. The patient had continued to drink after being arrested, but she reported that she now realized that she needed to go to a residential treatment center.

Mrs. M. completed a twenty-eight day detox and residential chemical dependency treatment program. She has been actively involved in an aftercare program, attends AA two or three times a week and has also continued to see the author in individual psychotherapy for over sixteen months. She has remained totally alcohol abstinent for nearly one year. After re-engaging in psychotherapy, Mrs. M. disclosed to me on several occasions how angry she had been with me for telling her, in effect, that she was an "alcoholic" and then trying to get her to see a physician, enter an inpatient treatment program and attend AA. She was "pissed" because she came to me for treatment and I basically conveyed to her at that point that I could not treat her!

This case presentation illustrates a basic example of how clients can respond in a generally negative or even self-defeating manner in response to the therapist's well intentioned self-disclosing behaviors and appropriate feedback. Mrs. M. responded to being told that she needed more extensive care by prematurely terminating her therapeutic relationship with the author. Fortunately, in this case, the client eventually entered an appropriate treatment program and re-engaged in individual psychotherapy. She has been actively and successfully engaged in the recovery process for several months. This case also demonstrates again how difficult it is to predict the impact of counselor self-disclosing behavior upon clients.

As noted earlier in this chapter, the client and the counselor's self-disclosing behaviors continually impact the therapeutic relationship in a diversity of constructive as well as potentially corrosive ways. Clinically and ethically appropriate counselor self-disclosures can simultaneously be very therapeutic as well as upsetting and disturbing to the client. Parataxic countertransference based therapist self-disclosures (Forrest, 2002) almost always have a destructive impact on the client and the therapeutic relationship. The capacity also always exists for counselors and therapists to make themselves emotionally upset by their personal self-disclosures in therapy. These situations almost axiomatically erode and contaminate the therapeutic alliance and the psychotherapeutic relationship.

The client's self-disclosures are also always potentially iatrogenic to the therapist, therapeutic alliance, and the therapeutic relationship. The potential for an iatrogenic effect specific to client self-disclosing behavior exists at every juncture in the therapeutic process. Therapists who work with chemically dependent, severely impulsive, antisocial, and more seriously disturbed patients or clients are especially vulnerable to the experience of being traumatized by the self-disclosing behaviors of the people they treat. The iatrogenic or psychonoxious impact of client self-disclosures upon therapists is also obviously enhanced by factors such as (1) the therapist's general mental and physical health, (2) the therapist's level of personal support, social adjustment, and general adjustment "outside" of his or her practice and career environment, (3) the duration, nature, and intensity of the therapist's professional career and work, and (4) other general life circumstances (i.e., financial status, marital and family adjustment across the lifespan, sources of collegial support, litigation issues, etc). Therapists who treat patient populations who consistently self-disclose about personal experiences involving long-term brutal physical, emotional, and sexual abuse are more prone to being emotionally damaged by their work than therapists who only listen to the self-disclosures of their far less emotionally conflicted "garden variety neurotic" clients. Therapists who limit their clinical work to individuals who manifest generalized anxiety, mild depression, periodic relational difficulties, career/vocational guidance, and situational adjustment problems are probably far less traumatized in the course of a short- or long-term clinical practice career than therapists who treat chemically dependent and other more pervasively or severely disturbed persons.

Finally, client and to a far lesser general extent therapist self-disclosures to the "self" can be psychonoxious as well as growth facilitating and curative. Honest and genuine client self-disclosures via self-dialogue or self-talk are often precursors to honest and genuine self-disclosures to the therapist and significant others. Many clients need to develop the capacity for *self*-disclosure, admittance, and confession (Hymer, 1988; Mowrer, 1961, 1964) and then begin the atonement process before they are able to be more open, self-disclosing, genuine, and consistently honest in their interactions with counselors and others. The process of disclosing to self may be very cathartic, self-enlightening, and therapeutic to begin with in a therapeutic relationship, or it can also be quite anxiety provoking, confusing, or depressing to the client. As the client and therapist interactively self-disclose within the context of an ongoing therapeutic relationship, these interactions generally foster progressively more transparency and authenticity upon the part of both participants. This includes an enhanced capacity for more in-depth and authentic disclosing to the self upon the part of the client as well as the therapist. This reciprocal process of disclosing more and more to self and others within the therapeutic relationship is essential to healthy client and therapist growth and personality change; however, this process can always potentially damage the client, therapist, or therapeutic relationship, and infrequently may actually facilitate a rupture of the therapeutic alliance.

Therapists and counselors need to remain aware, sensitive, and vigilant with regard to these various dynamics pertaining to self-disclosure in intensive psychotherapy and chemical dependency counseling throughout the course of their treatment relationships.

SUMMARY

This chapter examined the various therapeutic aspects of counselor and client self-disclosure in the specific realm of chemical dependency counseling. Clinically appropriate and well-timed therapist self-disclosures constitute an important ingredient in the therapeutic armamentarium of all chemical dependency counselors. Good therapist acumen always encompasses the sensitive, timely, and skillful use of personal self-disclosures throughout the course of intensive psychotherapeutic work with chemically dependent and substance-abusing persons.

The roles of therapist and client self-disclosure in the etiology and differential diagnosis of chemical dependency were briefly discussed in this chapter. These issues were also examined in greater depth in earlier chapters in the book. However, the actual therapy vignettes and case studies that were included in this chapter will enhance the readers understanding of the importance of therapist and client self-disclosure in these particular realms.

The bulk of this chapter examines the various parameters of therapist and client self-disclosure within the explicit realm of the chemical dependency counseling relationship and intensive therapy work with chemically dependent persons. Therapeutic and efficacious counselor or therapist self-disclosing behaviors pertaining to each of the stages of intensive chemical dependency counseling (Forrest, 1994, 1997, 2002, 2009) are delineated. Specific self-disclosure related therapist behaviors that are essential to the successful therapeutic process during each stage of intensive chemical dependency counseling and therapy are discussed. Case studies and therapy vignettes are also used to demonstrate the various therapeutic uses of counselor or therapist self-disclosure at various junctures in the process of intensive therapeutic work with these clients.

Finally, the impact of iatrogenic or potentially psychonoxious counselor and client self-disclosures in counseling and psychotherapy relationships with chemically dependent persons is addressed. Therapist and client self-disclosures in psychotherapy and chemically dependent counseling can always have a for better or worse impact on the therapist, client, or the therapeutic relationship. It was again noted in this chapter that it is always impossible to predict the precise effect of counselor and client self-disclosures in counseling and psychotherapy.

Effective counseling relationships are constructed via the openness and self-disclosures of clients and, to a lesser extent, therapists. The counseling and therapy relationship cannot develop, evolve, or become an effective vehicle for constructive personality growth and change in the absence of consistent and healthy self-disclosing behavior upon the part of the client and counselor. However, as discussed in this chapter, the client and counselor's self-disclosures can always potentially impact the therapeutic relationship in a diversity of psychonoxious ways. General sources of destructive therapist and client self-disclosure in therapy are identified in the chapter. A case study is also included in the chapter that demonstrates how therapist self-disclosures can adversely impact clients and the therapeutic alliance.

The parameters of client and therapist self-disclosure to the "self" and the more global aspects of self-disclosure as a mechanism of confession (Hymer, 1988; Mowrer, 1964) are also briefly discussed in the chapter.

This text will certainly help counselors and therapists become more aware of the importance and complexity of self-disclosure or transparency in counseling and psychotherapy. Healthy self-disclosure is a core ingredient in all effective psychotherapy relationships. Self-disclosure, transparency, and authenticity are also essential ingredients in optimal human adjustment. Effective counselors and therapists utilize myriad techniques to teach their chemically dependent clients more healthy self-disclosing behaviors.

Chapter 8

Client and Therapist Perspectives on Self-Disclosure and Recovery

INTRODUCTION

This text examines a plethora of professional issues associated with self-disclosure in psychotherapy and recovery. However, the general focus of the book encompasses research, clinical, and theoretical evidence as well as practice guidelines associated with these various professional issues. Earlier chapters explain historical and current theoretical positions pertaining to such topics as self-disclosure in counseling, psychotherapy, mental health, therapist theoretical-orientations related to self-disclosure, and the ethics of self-disclosure in psychotherapy. Clinical, research, theoretical and practice relevant findings, and evidence related to many other vicissitudes of therapist and client self-disclosure in professional therapeutic and self-help relationships were also discussed in earlier chapters.

Client and therapist perspectives on self-disclosure in psychotherapy and recovery constitute the focus of this chapter. The information and perspectives presented in this chapter are not based upon research or academic data and viewpoints. To the contrary, all of the information presented in chapter 8 is based upon the direct clinical experiences, observations, and viewpoints of several clients as well as clinical psychologists, psychiatrists, chemical dependency counselors and addictions specialists, graduate students, and social workers with whom the author has treated or worked with professionally over the past thirty-five years. The anonymity and confidentiality of former clients has been carefully maintained and guarded throughout the chapter. Therapist anonymity has also been maintained in the case of individuals wishing to remain anonymous.

The beliefs, experiences, and personal and professional viewpoints expressed on self-disclosure and recovery in this chapter are solely those of the contributors. The author and publisher have not modified or edited the basic opinions and viewpoints of the contributors to this chapter. These persons have shared their various sentiments, personal experiences, and viewpoints pertaining to self-disclosure in recovery, self-help programs, or professional psychotherapy relationships.

CLIENT PERSPECTIVES ON SELF-DISCLOSURE IN COUNSELING AND PSYCHOTHERAPY

I've been in and out of counseling for almost twenty years, and I've learned over the years that it isn't helpful if I'm not open or self-disclosing with my therapist. That can be hard to do, but as I've gotten older I can tell in a few sessions if I can open up to a therapist. It's all based on trust, and if you don't trust your therapist or feel safe with him (or her) in four or five sessions, I'd suggest getting a new one.

I spent the first ten or fifteen years of my therapy experiences with a bunch of therapists, always telling them "half-truths" and not being really open or disclosing. I've always had problems with being self-disclosing and really honest about my feelings . . . or anything else, until the last four years. I've been more open and self-disclosing with this therapist, and I've only had one therapist in the last five years and it's finally working. I haven't cut on myself in over eighteen months and for the first time ever . . . since I was eleven or twelve years old, I've been clean . . . no alcohol and drugs for over two years. It's the first time I ever went to AA (Alcoholics Anonymous) or had a sponsor for more than a few weeks. And I almost always look forward to group, and I've learned to be totally open in meetings and with my sponsor too. No more hiding stuff, lying, or telling the "half-truths." I've really never thought about it in this way but my openness and honest self-disclosures are cleansing. I'm not carrying all the emotional and past baggage shit anymore, and it's a lot easier to deal with myself and life . . . without drinking or cutting. My life isn't perfect but overall it's a lot better. Like we say in the program, life is more manageable.

I want to add that my last therapist has also been open and self-disclosing with me. I also feel it's really helped me a lot over the years. He's always shared about his recovery and problems, but he doesn't push his "stuff" on me. But I can remember him telling me a lot of times in the beginning that I wasn't being honest or self-disclosing with him or myself. He wanted me to be honest and share my feelings and experiences in our sessions and he's always said "it's hard to bullshit a bullshitter." I don't think I've ever been able to get anything over on him and he's held me accountable.

One thing I have seen in the program is that the people who don't open up and share or get involved don't usually hang around. . . . I mean they drop out, and I don't think they stay sober either. That applies to women and men. It's not just women. But I don't know if that applies to therapy? Maybe people who aren't ready or able to be open or self-disclosing to their therapist's drop out too? At least in my case, I know that I didn't start to get better, and I sure didn't stay clean until I was able to be open and honest . . . rigorously honest like you hear in the program with my therapist and sponsor and other people in the program. It seems like a lot of addicts have problems with being honest about themselves and especially with talking about their pasts.

Mary C.

My name is Dave and I'm a recovering alcoholic. I've been sober for over thirty-two years. Not one drink in thirty-two years! I found my sobriety in AA, but after being hospitalized for three weeks following a near fatal car wreck . . . thirty-two years ago caused by my drinking. I still go to two or three AA meetings a week after all these years and I'm active in the program . . . with sponsoring people, service work, and attending conventions and workshops. If I understand what you mean by the term "self-disclosure," it's crucial to recovery. That's because all alcoholics lie about their drinking, and they'll go to any lengths to cover it up, deny it, and never honestly discuss their disease with themselves, let alone others. That's how it is when they're drinking and until they are really ready to stop.

Let's face it, a lot of alcoholics never develop the capacity to get honest with themselves and others, and it's been my experience that they're also the ones who don't self-disclose. They're the people who can't talk to their family, spouse, or sponsor. I've known a lot of them who tried to see a counselor or were forced to go to counseling. They either don't talk with these other people, or they always try to tell them what they think they want to hear.

Pain is at the heart of this issue to me. I had to deal with myself, and I've listened to it and seen it in the lives of hundreds of other addicts and alcoholics. We can't talk about our childhoods, feelings, and lives because of all the pain and emotional hell we've experienced. For a lot of us, it seems like it never ends. It's all we've known and it hurts like hell, and is embarrassing to talk about with others. Our natural instinct is to deny it, hope it'll go away, and never talk about it. My father was a drunk and I can still remember the beatings and unending hell he put us all through. And I was becoming just like him the last year or two before I got into the program.

Once you get sober and begin down the road of recovery, you've got to continue to talk openly with others about everything. Self-disclosure and continuing to disclose to your sponsor or therapist, and maybe above all, to yourself and your higher power will help you keep your sobriety. It is one day at a time and it's sure worked for me. I didn't share or disclose my personal "business" with anyone before I got involved in the program of Alcoholics Anonymous. One thing I've learned for sure over the past thirty-two years is that I don't have to carry all that stuff inside myself. I get rid of it by talking about it and sharing it with others. And I think that is what self-disclosure is all about!

Dave R.

Talking about yourself to other was something we never did in our family. I can remember Mom and Dad both telling me over and over again when I was a little girl to keep our "business" in the family. That meant that we never told our neighbors, friends, or even relatives about anything that was going on in our family. I didn't tell my best friends what was going on in "our" home, and my parents and older brother never talked openly about anything either.

I think I knew that both of my parents were drunks when I was eight or nine years old, but I definitely knew they were alcoholics in junior high. Dad was drunk every night and Mom wasn't far behind. They really hit it each weekend. Bobby and I knew when they were pissed off or angry because they yelled, threw things, and fought a lot. Looking back, is seems like they really didn't have any friends or social relationships outside of the family by the time I was in the ninth or tenth grade, and I sure wasn't about to bring any of my friends . . . boys or other girls to our house. You never knew what it would be like at any time. Sometimes they weren't fighting and it seemed to be okay, but ten minutes later and they would be crazy, and Dad hit her more than once. I sure didn't want my friends to see what was going on in our home and I felt embarrassed and shame.

The other thing I remember about being open with others or the self-disclosure topic is that our family had a lot of secrets. We knew it as kids and we learned to keep those secrets to ourselves. I still have to work on not keeping secrets.

All of the covering up, keeping secrets, and not disclosing stuff to myself or others began to change for me when I started going to AA and NA. That's only been three years now and I'm twenty-five years old, and I've been married twice and my son is six years old. And quite frankly, all the openness and self-disclosure I was exposed to in recovery scared the shit out of me at first. I couldn't believe the stories and real stuff I heard in those first few meetings, and I was always anxious about hearing it at first. But I also figured out pretty fast that I felt better and was less stressed when I started to open up and participate in the meetings. It got easier the longer I went to meetings, and when I finally had enough courage to get a sponsor, we started meeting together every week or so, and she shared or was totally open with me, and I think I really began to learn how to open-up and disclose to her. I disclosed everything to her and I actually did my inventory with her, and we've worked on Big Book issues and the steps for over two years now. And it must be working. I've been clean and sober for over two years now.

I think you've got to be ready to open up to someone. I know I tried counseling a couple of months after I started to go to meetings, but I wasn't ready to open up or disclose my feelings and experiences to the counselor then. Maybe it was because I still wanted to use or drink, but looking back I also just couldn't open up to him about all of the pain and emotional horrors I had experienced in my family. I had never talked about those things to anyone, and the sexual stuff with my brother didn't come out until I started to do the step work with my sponsor. She was another woman and her step-dad sexually abused her when she was ten to twelve years old. We had some core issues in common and I couldn't talk about that issue with the counselor. Not then and I'm not sure I'm ready to begin dealing with that issue yet or, for that matter, a number of other one's with a therapist.

Carla T.

My take on the self-disclosure and recovery issue is that it's pretty important in recovery and therapy, but I'm still not real comfortable with the idea of discussing my personal life with anybody. That's probably why I haven't been able to stay sober. I'm feeling better, and I've got almost six months this time but I spent ninety days in a half-way home this time and I completed a twenty-eight day program about a year before that. I can remember getting out of treatment the first time. I was real gung-ho and felt great for a month or two, and then I ended up drunk again and got a DUI. I also remember that I didn't want anything to do with a sponsor, and the only reason I saw Dr. W. in therapy when I left treatment is that my counselor at the treatment center told me I really needed to get in therapy. I didn't really want it myself.

When I think back to my therapy a year ago, I really resented it when my therapist tried to get me to open up. He pissed me off a couple of times, and I pretty much told him and the group that I felt the self-disclosure stuff . . . especially in the group, was inappropriate. I guess I still feel that my personal life or experiences, feelings too, are my business . . . they're private and nobody else's. I've never wanted to talk about being adopted, I can remember that issue since I was six or seven years old. And my step-parents have been great.

Thinking about it, I guess I'm still pretty ambivalent about disclosing to people in the program, but I can talk to my sponsor now. At least I'm going to meetings and my wife and I are really having problems again. I'm open to seeing a marriage counselor, but I've still got the mixed feelings about the self-disclosure thing with a therapist. I've agreed to go to a counselor with her, but it's still going to be hard for me to really open up with them and get honest about all the shit in my life.

But deep down, I still think I know that I've got to start opening-up or disclosing to my wife and sponsor at least. In my head I guess I know that self-disclosure is important for recovery, but at least now I know that I'm still working on that piece of my recovery program. One day at a time!

Bob B.

I've just started seeing a counselor and I've only been in the program for about fourteen months . . . this time, but it's the longest I've ever been clean and sober since I was eleven or twelve years old . . . that's after about twelve years of using anything I could get my hands on. Hello, real world!

If I understand what Dr. Forrest means by self-disclosure, I'd say that it is probably a big part of me being able to put together some real recovery time for a change. I had to see a counselor for awhile after I got my first DUI, and Billy and I tried marriage counseling a couple of times in 2004 but we were both screwed up all the time . . . and he was worse that me, plus being a professional "bullshitter."

I just hope I can keep workin' the program and I don't want to go back. . . . I've got to keep some of the past in the front of my head so I don't repeat it again. I've been down the relapse road too many times. It seems to me that I've been more . . . a lot more disclosing this time . . . to everyone, and I've tried to be really open up and be honest with my sponsor and I'm trying with my new counselor.

She's (client's counselor) a "normie," but she seems to understand and she is easy to open to. I know I've got to be honest too. I think the program has finally helped me to start being more open about all kinds of things . . . not just my past feelings and experiences, but I'm really trying to get honest with myself and others.

Tammy W.

First of all, I've been given several diagnoses over the past ten or fifteen years . . . like bipolar, depression, anxiety, borderline personality, antisocial, and alcoholic. I got into a lot of different drugs and alcohol when I was seventeen or eighteen and until I was probably thirty, but I've been out of all the drugs except for alcohol for about ten years . . . I know that I'm an alcoholic because it's gotten to the point over the last few years that I get in trouble or end up back in jail every time I drink. I think I'm accepting that I'm bipolar now too, but I don't know about the other ones. My psychiatrist at the state hospital pretty much convinced me about the bipolar. I got that diagnosis a long time ago too. After another three months in another inpatient program I feel like I'm really starting to get better. I've been clean and sober for almost two years; I'm still in therapy and going to meetings every other day, and I haven't missed one meeting with my shrink . . . plus I've had a sponsor in the program for almost a year and no more hassles with the cops or my "ex," and I'm doin' a lot better with my folks.

Trying to look back, I know deep down that this is the first time I ever really committed myself to treatment or recovery, and this is darned sure the first time I ever got honest and talked about my real issues to anyone. Before it was always 90 percent horseshit with me. I didn't disclose anything to anybody else or myself, and when I did it was always half-truths at best. Maybe I wasn't capable of being honest or self-disclosing in the past but for whatever reason . . . maybe because I'm sober and still takin' my meds, I'm trying to be more open or disclosing and "rigorously" honest with everybody, including me.

I think basic honesty is more important than self-disclosure. But they go together to help you get better. It's not just staying sober. I know I've got a lot of other problems too, and now it's easier to be more disclosing about any of it.

Mike Z.

BUN'S STORY

In 1966, I found myself in an organization called Alcoholics Anonymous. How I got there is quite an interesting story. I was born in the little mining town of Leadville, Colorado, in 1923. My dad passed away in 1930, and my mother was left to raise four boys, the oldest of which at the time was sixteen and I was the youngest at six.

This happened at the height of the so-called Depression and times were pretty tough, but my mother managed to hold things together, and we at least got a high school education.

I graduated from high school in June, 1941, and the following December the Japanese bombed Pearl Harbor, which brought on World War II. I entered the service in June, 1943, and served the next two and half year in the army, field artillery; two years of which were served in the Southwest Pacific, a year in New Guinea and a year in the Philippines. I rose to the rank of Master Sergeant and was awarded several decorations, including the Bronze Star Medal. August, 1945 saw us preparing to hit the Home Islands of Japan when the United State unleashed the atomic bombs on Hiroshima and Nagasaki, which essentially brought an end to the war. After serving in the occupation of Japan, I was honorably discharged in January, 1946, and returned to civilian life. I think its pretty ironic that in 1949, I would end up in Los Alamos, New Mexico, working right alongside some of the people who had developed the atomic weapons and whom I felt might have saved my life because only God knows how many of us would have survived the invasion of Japan.

In the fall of 1961, I decided to leave my employment with the Los Alamos National Laboratory and take over the ownership of a local bar and restaurant known as the Carriage Inn. This turned out to be a disaster. I had a wife and two children (a boy and a girl) to support, and in less than four years' time I had turned the Carriage Inn into the Mis-Carriage Inn. I had become my own best customer. The business was down the drain, creditors were calling every day, I had a wife with a kid in each hand ready to walk, and I ended up in the Los Alamos Medical Center with what the doctors called a perforated ulcer. But I now know this was nothing but alcoholic gastritis. Up until this time I had always been a big man physically; weighing anywhere from 190 pounds to 210 pounds. At the time, fast pitch softball was one of our most popular sports. I was clocked throwing the ball at one hundred miles per hour; good enough that I got to pitch in seven world tournaments and was the pitcher for a five-man exhibition team (Pierotti's Clowns) that raised thousands of dollars for different charities.

It's November 1965 and I have been in this Medical Center for seven weeks. I have undergone three surgeries, lost two-thirds of my digestive track, and gone from 190 pounds to 128 pounds. Two weeks out of the hospital and I'm right back drinking again. The insanity of this addiction to alcohol is beyond imagination. The drinking went on for the next couple of months and the last weekend in January, 1966, turned out to be my last drink. I got up on a Sunday morning after a weekend of drinking, looked in the mirror, and could no longer stand what I was seeing. That's the day I called a friend who was a member of Alcoholics Anonymous, and that's the day my life changed for the better. In my opinion, the twelve steps of Alcoholic Anonymous is the greatest design for living that anyone has ever come up with. In February of this year, 2006, I achieved forty years of sobriety, but to describe forty years of sobriety is impossible. You have to live it to understand it. It has truly been an adventure! The friends I have made, the things I have gotten to do would fill a book, and all because I found this program.

My wife, seeing me make a move toward AA, decided to hang around and see if it would work. She hung around for fifty-four years and died very suddenly and very unexpectedly three years ago, and the thought to take a drink never crossed my mind. Both children were raised, educated, and are doing very well for themselves.

In closing, all I can say is "thank God for 1966" and "thank God for Alcoholics Anonymous." These disclosures have been essential to my recovery and personal growth over the past forty years, and I would also like to believe that I have helped others in the program with their recoveries through my own honest self-disclosures.

FRANK A'S STORY: WHAT IT USED TO BE LIKE, WHAT HAPPENED, AND WHAT IT IS LIKE NOW: A PERSONAL AA-BASED PERSPECTIVE ON SELF-DISCLOSURE AND RECOVERY

Once an alcoholic always an alcoholic; an alcoholic can never successfully drink again.

> Hi, my name is Frank A. and I am an alcoholic. My sobriety date is 23 March 1975. I am retired army and federal civilian service.
>
> I was born and raised in the small country farming town of Clinton, North Carolina, and I am the youngest of seven brothers and sisters. My dad was an alcoholic and so was his dad. Five out of my brothers and sisters were alcoholics. My dad, his dad, two brothers, and two sisters died from the disease of alcoholism.
>
> My first drink was at the age of four and a half, and before I was ten years old I was making my own wine from wild berries I got from the woods.
>
> During my junior high school years and high school I did not drink. I loved sports, and if you played any school sports you were not allowed to drink. I played high school baseball and always went out for the high school football team.
>
> My goal when I graduated from high school was to teach physical education and health sciences.
>
> I came from a poor family and could not afford to go to college because my father became unable to work. I began supporting my parents when I was

fifteen years old. My brothers and sisters had married and left home before I started first grade. I was raised like an only child because of this.

The part of town I was raised in was like the "other side of the railroad tracks." I did not want my school friends to know were I lived.

At that time, the Boy Scouts took Saturday road marches past my home, and when I saw them coming past my house, I would run and hide so they would not see me. But one day I did not run fast enough and one of them caught me. He was one of my classmates and he was thirsty and wanted a drink of water. The house my parents lived in had no running water or inside toilet. We had an outhouse and my mom cooked on a wood-burning stove that I used to cut the wood for. We stayed warm from a wood-burning stove!

So when I took this Boy Scout and classmate into our house, I had to pump the water out of the ground with a hand pump. When he drank the water he stated it was the best water he had ever tasted, and after that we became good friends and I no longer felt like an outsider.

I really enjoyed high school and sports and I became one of the team.

When I graduated from school, I won a one-year scholarship to East Carolina University, but there were other family financial problems and my father was still unable to work. As a result, I could not afford to go to college.

But then I figured out how to do both. Join the army and the army would pay for my education and also help me take care of my parents. So I joined the army.

From eighth grade until I graduated I had not gotten into the alcohol. I could take it or leave it at that time. All through school and until about 1956–57, I was also not into the girlfriend thing. I had female friends but no girlfriends.

When I went into the army is when I began getting into the drinking. I drank because that is what the rest of my army buddies did. I am not saying any of them were, or are, alcoholics. I went through a part of my military career when I could "take it or leave it."

I got out of the army in August, 1956, and went back home to try to make a go of it. My goal at that time was to go to college and support my parents, but when I got back home the tobacco fields, cotton patches, sacking groceries, and pumping gas were still the only jobs available. I tried it but things were no different than when I went into the army in 1953 after I got out of high school.

I tried for about eighteen months to find a good job, but nothing seemed to work. I still was not into the drinking at that time. So I decided I would go back into the military. This time I went into the air force in February, 1958. My first real duty assignment in the air force was the Aleutian Islands of Alaska. We had one building on the entire island! It was the building where I ate, slept, and worked with about twenty-five people. We had our own club and bar, but I still could control my drinking during that tour of duty.

I was separated from the AF in March, 1961, and I went back home again to see if I could make it on the outside—in civilian life. I was soon drunk more often than not. I had almost forgotten my goals from high school: to teach physical education and health sciences.

When I got out of the AF nothing really had changed in my hometown. The tobacco fields and cotton patches were still there.

But this time I met a girl. We dated for over a year and in July, 1962, we got married. I was ten years older, and financially things went well for awhile. I had a job and still had to support my mom. My dad had passed away in 1959.

Like I said, things went well financially for awhile, and then things began to crumble. Here I go again, I said to myself, "I know who will take care of me and my family." I went back into the army in September, 1963, until I retired in July, 1977.

I took basic training all over again at Ft. Jackson, South Carolina. My next duty station was Ft. Bragg, North Carolina. I signed in at Ft. Bragg the day John F. Kennedy was assassinated.

I stayed at Ft. Bragg from November 1963 until July 1965. My wife was pregnant with a daughter that was born on May 19, 1965.

In May 1965 I came down on levy to go to Germany. Because of my rank in the army, I was not eligible for concurrent travel, so I had to go to Germany alone, find a place to live, and then send for my wife. I went to Germany and in October 1965, I sent for my wife and new baby. In October, 1965, my wife arrived in Stuttgart Germany. I picked her up at the airport and took her and our daughter to the apartment I had rented. The same evening my wife and daughter arrived in Germany, as we were sitting at the dinner table, my wife looked at me and said, "Frank I do not love you anymore; I am going home." She had been in Germany for no more than three or four hours and dropped a bomb on me. "I want a divorce and the baby and I are going back home to Clinton, North Carolina."

This was on a Saturday. The day before I picked her up from the airport, I bought a fifth of Jim Beam. After she told me this, I started to drink the Jim Beam and I did not stop until it was gone. This was when I lost control of my drinking. And from that day on I drank on a daily basis. I put her on a plane on 9 November, 1965, two days before my birthday on November 11, 1965. And I started a life alone and all by myself. I lived in the barracks at the time and went nowhere other than to work and my room. I kept bottles in my car; I got drunk daily. I felt sorry for myself and was always on the pity pot. This was not supposed to happen to me. When you took wedding vows at that time the preacher said, "till death do us part." These were the same vows my mom and dad took; no matter how bad it got, you lived with it, not like it is today.

As I said, I lived in the barracks, went nowhere except to my room after work, felt sorry for myself, wrote letters to my wife telling her "let's give it another try," and drank.

I had a roommate who became tired of my feeling sorry for myself and one day he got fed up with it and said, "when you get off work tonight you better be dressed because I am getting you out of the barracks, and stop feeling sorry for yourself." That evening I was dressed and I went out with him to a German house and drank the night away. And from that day on it was always going out drinking to forget.

On New Years Eve of 1966, I dated my present wife for the first time. She had gotten my attention from other places I drank, so I asked her for a date, and it was for a New Years party at the NCO Club in Germany.

I continued to drink and to date my present wife on a regular basis. In March of 1967, I asked her to marry me because I was due to go back to the states in July, 1967, but I was still married to my first wife. I asked my first wife to send me the divorce papers and I would sign them. She did and in July, 1967, I got on one plane and my German girlfriend got on another, and we met in JFK in New York. We drove to my home in North Carolina a day or so later, went to Aiken, South Carolina, and were married. And this is the best thing I believe I have ever done. I married my current wife and stopping drinking. Without her I do not believe I would be where I am in life today.

I continued to drink, but with a little more control.

My next duty station was Ft. Polk, Louisiana, with a new wife and some happy times, but the drinking continued.

May 1968, ten months after I got back stateside, I came down on levy again but this time it was to Vietnam. My new wife did not speak English too well, and now I was leaving her alone in the United States, and she was eight months pregnant. Our plan was to move to Augusta, Georgia. I had a brother there who would help look out for her while I was in Vietnam. When I left for Vietnam I had a new addition to the family, our daughter, Christina, who was thirty days old when I left.

I had an idea that there was something wrong with my drinking for a long time, and I said to myself "this will be a good time to do something about my drinking—a combat area, no drinking and I can get a handle on it." So I left for Vietnam with this plan.

When I got to Vietnam, the soldier who I was to replace was so glad to see me, he said, "Let's go to the club and I will buy you a drink." And for an alcoholic, that was a great idea! I took that drink and never drew a sober breath the whole time I was in Vietnam.

When I returned home from Vietnam there were no bands or people to cheer for me when I got off the plane, like it is today; the only person there to take me home was my wife.

My wife knew I liked Jim Beam and she bought a fifth of Jim Beam a month while I was gone and put it in the hallway closet. When I got home there were twelve fifths of Jim Bean just waiting for me! In less than a month those twelve fifths were gone, not including the two I used to chase them with.

I went to Ft. Gordon, Georgia, in August, 1969, assigned to the Army Signal School and was a dining facility manager. I continued to drink on a daily basis and during duty hours. My drinking didn't create any duty problems at that time because it was kind of acceptable to come to work hungover and there was someone to cover for me.

This pattern of drinking continued for the next ten months, and then I came down on levy for Germany again in June/July, 1970.

For the first time since we were married, I took my wife home to see her parents, and they were also able to see their granddaughter for the first time.

We got to Germany the 1 of August, 1970, and on the 21 of August the Red Cross informed me that my mom had died, and I was immediately on a plane to go to my mom's funeral. My brother picked me up at the airport and before we left to go home, we stopped to pick up a twelve pack of beer. It was gone before we got home, thirty-five miles away. The whole month I was gone for my mom's funeral neither I nor my brother drew a sober breath.

After the funeral, I went back to Germany to serve the rest of my three-year tour of duty.

January 1, 1971, was the beginning of the all-volunteer army, and the army wanted to glamorize the army. They put beer machines in the barracks and put machines in the dining facilities, every one but mine. Instead, they went to a local brewery, bought enough beer to fill a fifteen hundred square-foot room to the ceiling, and gave me the only key to the room. That puts an alcoholic in hog heaven! Beer was to be sold in the dining facility at the evening meal. Every morning I would go to the beer room and do an inventory, and naturally I had to taste it to make sure it was good enough for human consumption. That is what dining facility managers do. Food has to be good enough for human consumption!

My chain of command at that time thought I was drinking on duty but could not do anything about it because everyone was doing it. Two-beer lunches were authorized, but they kept trying to catch me doing something wrong. They weren't able to.

This went on from about April to May, 1973. In May, I was to go to the NCO Academy, and the chain of command thought I could not make it through the academy. And if I didn't, they could separate me from the army without my retirement. I had about fifteen to sixteen years in the military at that time. But, I fooled them and I made it. I graduated. But, while I was in the NCO Academy my drinking did not slow down.

During the last couple weeks of the academy, my daughter, Chrisy, was diagnosed with cystic fibrosis. I did not dare drop out of the academy, but I could have PCS'd back to the United States because of my daughter's diagnosis. I stayed, graduated, and then was processed to return stateside early so she could get treatment.

My next duty station and my last while on active duty was Ft. Carson, Colorado.

When I arrived at Ft. Carson, I knew something was wrong with my drinking, but I could not believe I was an "alcoholic." I was going to try to change and work on it, but as it turned out again, everywhere I would go I took the alcoholism with me. No matter where I would go, it seemed like alcoholics attracted each other.

I continued to drink out of control, and the first thing in my life that the alcohol was affecting was my marriage and family. It did not bother the army that your marriage and family was falling apart; they used to say, "If we wanted you to have a house, a wife, or family, we would issue one."

My drinking did not begin to affect my duty performance until August/ September, 1974. Somewhere around that time my wife began calling the CDR and 1st sergeant and telling them I had a drinking problem and they needed to do something about it. And when she would call my commander/1st sergeant, one of them would come over to the dining facility to check me out. But when they came, they were never close enough to smell me. I covered up my drinking in the army by being one of the best looking soldiers in the army: spit shinned boots, hair cut, and being where I was supposed to be when I was supposed to be and doing what I was supposed to be doing! They would go back to the orderly room, call my wife and tell her, "There is nothing wrong with your husband; he is where he is supposed to be, doing what he is supposed to be doing, and he is one of the sharpest soldiers in the unit." This went on several times but I was never confronted about my drinking.

In August 1974, we had a change of command. I guess the old commander must have informed the new commander that "he had "better look out for SFC Austin; he may have a drinking problem." The new commander came over to the dining facility at one of the lunch meals, and he came into my kitchen where I was helping set up the serving line and confronted me. He stated, "I understand that you may have a drinking problem, and if you do you better do something about it or else I am giving you a one-way ticket home and you ain't coming back." I had nineteen years in the army and he was threatening to throw me out before my retirement. I said to the commander, "Let me think about it for awhile and maybe I'll go to the alcohol treatment program here at Ft. Carson."

He left my kitchen; I jumped up and down like a kid, pouted, went out to my car and took a drink. That is how much his statement affected me.

My drinking continued. On the 13th of October, 1974, we were informed that we would be moving out on a division readiness exercise on Monday the 16th of October. That Friday, I got my cooks together and we loaded the mess truck so on Monday when they blew the whistle we would be ready to go. When Monday came we served breakfast, cleaned the mess hall, and were sitting around waiting to be informed that it was time to go. I began going through "the shakes" and alcohol withdrawal, and I needed a drink bad. I had to find a drink! So I left the area to find a drink and when I got back to the mess hall everyone was gone. I had missed our movement on a division readiness exercise and it was late in the afternoon.

I looked around and no one was left but me, and I looked up and saw an army truck heading towards the field. I threw my TA50 over my shoulder and started running to catch the truck. The driver must have seen me in the rear view mirror and he stopped. I threw my stuff on the truck, jumped up on the truck, and low and behold, there were about ten to fifteen chopper pilots on the truck. I knew they could smell the alcohol on me from about three blocks away, but no one said anything to me about my drinking. We got to the training area and my cooks had already served two meals and were packing to go to the exercise area, and I strolled around the area like a big shot, like a lot of high ranking people. Yet no one said anything to me about drinking.

We got to the exercise area and set up the mess tent and got ready for the next day. I told my cooks to go hit the sack. I would take care of the things that needed to be taken care of because they had a long, rough day.

Somewhere around 9 p.m. that evening the commander finally made it to the field and one of the first places he came to was the mess area to get a cup of coffee and his meal. I knew he was only two to three feet from me and he could smell me, but he said nothing about my drinking. This was the same commander who had stated a month or so earlier, "If you don't do something about your drinking, you are out."

I struggled on through that night and was up early the next morning ready to serve breakfast at 6:00–6:30 a.m. Somewhere about that same time, the dining facility officer came to the mess tent and stated to me, "SFC Austin, get your stuff; we are going back to garrison." I said, "What for? I just got here." He said, "Just get your things; we are going back." None of what had happened the day before crossed my mind. The only thing that entered my mind was I had left and the SFC back in garrison had to take care of the people that were left behind. The only thing I could think of was that he had accused me of was stealing some of his food and taking it with me to the field. Before we left the field. I stepped into the woods and got me a stick about the size of a baseball bat and I said to myself. "I'll fix that SOB for accusing me of stealing."

When we got back to garrison and parked in the back of the mess hall, I jumped out of the truck with my stick, went into the kitchen, and I was going to knock the hell out of that guy for accusing me of stealing. But before I could get through the kitchen, the mess officer stopped me and said, "SFC Austin, he has not accused you of anything." Then I asked, "What in the hell are we doing here?" He replied, "You and I are going to see the command sergeant major" and that is when all that had happened the day before came back to me and I said to myself, "Oh shit!" The mess officer took me to see the CSM, and the command sergeant major took me by the hand, put me into his VW Beetle, and took me to the Ft. Carson Alcohol Treatment program. The commander proceeded to enter me into their three week inpatient program.

All of this upset me. "What are they doing to me? I'm not an alcoholic," I said to myself. When they put me in the treatment program, I said to myself, "I am only going to do whatever it takes to get these people off my back and when the time is right, I am going to drink." I had no intention of stopping. This was on the 17th of October, 1974. I was put into treatment and I'll never forget that date as long as I live.

I completed the Ft. Carson inpatient program on November 9, 1974, and drank on my way home after being released. I stopped by a package store and got a few shot bottles of vodka.

I did not want to go back to my unit because I did not know what to expect or who would be out to get me. I was constantly looking over my shoulder to see who was watching me.

All I was going to do was just enough to get my wife, the commander, and 1st sergeant off my back, and when I got out of treatment the only requirement was go to four to five AA (Alcoholic Anonymous) meetings weekly and one weekly group counseling session.

I would go the meetings, drinking in between, but not to the extreme as before.

I controlled my drinking pretty well up to about mid-February, 1975. Things were going good at home, things were going good at work, and Frank said, "Now is the time," and I picked up a " big drunk" and it lasted until March 22, 1975.

On the morning of March 22, 1975, I was backing out of my drive way at 4 a.m. to go to Ft. Carson to open my dining facility like I had been doing for years. The minute the tail end of my car hit the street in front of my house, I went into a "blackout." The next thing I could remember of the day was 10:30 that night. When I came out of the blackout, I found myself locked in a toilet and couldn't remember how I got there. My wife had been to the toilet door several times, knocking, banging, trying to get me to come out, but I didn't. When I came out of that blackout, I was scared to death. So many things rushed through my head. I could have been driving through my neighborhood, run over a neighbor kid, and killed some people or myself. I was scared to death. If I did not learn anything else while in I was in treatment, I did learn one thing: I am responsible for my behaviors no matter what condition I am in. Drunk or sober, I am responsible for my behavior. Because I had learned that when I put alcohol in my body, the blackouts could happen. I had experienced many blackouts before, but not for that length of time.

My wife had been involved in Al-Anon for a year and half to two years before my last drink. My drinking had made her as sick as I was, and she needed a support group to help her cope with my drinking and live with me. Why she stayed with me during that time, I do not know. She loved me that much, I guess. While I was still in the blackout she remembered somewhere from her Al-Anon program something we do in AA that is called "twelve stepping." This is when a recovering alcoholic goes out and helps other suffering alcoholics. She thought, "Maybe that will work for Frank." She went upstairs to the kitchen, found the Colorado Springs telephone directory, and turned to the yellow pages. Under the A's she found Alcoholics Anonymous. She dialed the twenty-four-hour hotline, told them of the possible condition I was in, and asked if they'd send someone to my home to talk with me. Somewhere about the time I came out of that eighteen-and-a-half-hour blackout, around 10:30 p.m., an AA member was knocking on my front door, ready to give me a helping hand if I wanted it. I do not believe I wanted help any more in my life than I wanted it then. I was scared to death, and I knew something had to change or else I was going to die. Hal N. from AA twelve-stepped me that night. He stayed with me from approximately 10:30 p.m. until almost 3 a.m. trying to tell me what I was doing to myself as a result of my drinking. He said, "Frank, you're killing yourself and you do not want to die, do you?" At that point in my military career, I was only two months away from my twenty years and I could retire, and I did not want to die. I may have drunk a lot those last seven to eight years of my military career, but I believed that I earned that retirement. And I wanted to enjoy some of that retirement I felt I had earned!

As I mentioned earlier, when I came out of the blackout, I was scared to death. I served a year in Vietnam and was never as scared in Vietnam as I was the night of my last drunk. So many things rushed through my head: driving through the neighborhood, killing one of the kids, or an accident on Academy Blvd, perhaps even killing a bunch of people.

On the 23 of March, 1975, I just started doing some of the things that had been suggested to me some six months before by my counselor, Wanda. She suggested I go to AA, take antabuse, and start keeping my appointments with her. Before my last drunk, I just went to AA to get the heat off my back—my wife, my chain of command—and to get my card punched. On the 23rd of March, 1975, I began going to AA because I wanted to get better, I took antabuse and kept my appointments with my counselor. And I haven't found it necessary to take a drink since that night Hal N. from AA "twelve-stepped" me. But I did it because I finally wanted to stop drinking for me and no one else. And, as I eventually learned, if I do it for myself, I automatically do it for others.

When I started doing those four things—attending AA, taking antabuse, keeping my appointments, and doing if for me—my life began to change. Here it is March 23, 2007, thirty- four years later, and I still haven't found it necessary to drink.

When I retired from the army in 1977, I went to Pikes Peak Community College in Colorado Springs to earn a counseling degree. October of 1977, I got a job at Pikes Peak Mental Health working in an inpatient alcohol treatment facility. In 1979, I earned my associates degree from PPCC, and in 1980 I began work in an army alcohol/drug treatment program. I began working on my bachelor's degree at the University of Southern Colorado, and I earned my masters degree in substance abuse in 1984. I love working with alcoholics and addicts. I did that almost from the day I got sober. I was told when I stopped drinking that, "in order to keep it (sobriety and recovery), you have to give it away." That is what Hal N. and many other recovering alcoholics also told me.

But it doesn't mean because I stopped drinking, life has been a bowl of cherries. It has not been. My daughter who had cystic fibrosis passed away in April, 1998, and I was diagnosed with throat cancer in 2000. With radiation treatment I overcame that, but in 2003 I was diagnosed with lung cancer. However, I haven't found it necessary to take a drink. Why? Because Frank did not like the old Frank; he was not a very nice person.

Also as a result of treatment, people like Doc Forrest, and the fellowship of Alcoholics Anonymous, I have been able to stay sober and in active recovery.

But it all began in December 1934 when Bill Wilson, Cofounder of Alcoholics Anonymous was released from the hospital after his last drunk and DTs and probably felt the best he had felt in ages. He told his wife, Lois, when they got home that he liked the feeling he was having. He also told Lois, "Maybe I can stay sober by helping other alcoholics get sober." This is still the philosophy of Alcoholics Anonymous almost seventy years later. Trying to help other alcoholics, stay sober one day at a time, and encourage them to go to meetings.

I know I am only one drink away from a drunk. Do I want to go through that experience again? No because I do not know if I can survive another drunk. I do not know if I would be able to get to another AA meeting, a hospital, or a treatment facility. I have learned since my last drink that there is nothing so bad going on in my life that a drink won't make worse, and I would not want to start all over. Once an alcoholic, always an alcoholic. Today, I am recovering one day at a time.

The past thirty-four years of my life have been the best years of my life because I wasted the first forty in a bottle. And I thank people like Gary Forrest, who I look at like being my mentor, and the people in Alcoholics Anonymous for showing me the way.

My recovery story is based upon self-disclosure. As a recovering alcoholic and a counselor, I know that self-disclosure helps people get sober and change. By disclosing my story to hundreds of alcoholics and addicts over all these years, I have helped myself and others recover. We share our experiences, strength, and hope with each other so that we may solve our common problems and help others recover from alcoholism.

The people who recover from this disease always learn to disclose their stories to others. We stay drunk and sick until we begin to get honest and self-disclosing with ourselves and others. Self-disclosure helps recovery become a possibility for every alcoholic.

Frank A., BS, MA

THERAPIST PERSPECTIVES ON SELF-DISCLOSURE IN COUNSELING AND PSYCHOTHERAPY

As a practicing psychiatrist for over twenty years, I can't overemphasize how important it is for patients and their families to be self-disclosing and honest with me about their various symptoms and, for that matter, many other issues pertaining to their lives. Psychiatry, general medicine, and the other behavioral health professions are basically like detective work. We can be very limited in our diagnostic and treatment efforts when we lack information or receive misinformation from patients and their families. Moreover, a sizeable segment of psychiatric and certainly drug-abusing patients simply don't tell the truth about their symptoms and lives. Some can be so emotionally disturbed or drug dependent that they are unable to disclose or experience great difficulty disclosing their symptoms, feelings, or thoughts.

Psychiatrists and physicians have long been trained to be non-disclosing. Psychiatrists and especially psychoanalysts or analytically-trained psychiatrists were taught to basically never self-disclose to their patients. This has changed a great deal over the last twenty-five years, but we're still trained to be listeners who make timely or strategic interpretations. The issue of therapist or psychiatrist self-disclosure remains a thorny and disputed or controversial issue in psychiatry training programs as well as psychiatric practice. However, Dr. Forrest's book and other recent publications continue to advance our knowledge and help practitioners with these issues. Patient self-disclosure is the relatively simple part of the self-disclosure equation. A lack of consistent patient self-disclosing behavior that is forthright, accurate, and honest equates with diagnostic inaccuracies and always, later if not sooner, poor treatment outcomes, for psychiatric patients. This can be even truer for patients who are being treated for various other medical conditions.

I have become progressively more open and self-disclosing with my patients over the past twenty-five years, and I believe that I have become a more effective clinician in all or my roles as a result of this openness. In general, we need to be more disclosing with our patients about treatment expectations, medications, care alternatives, and even poor outcomes or treatment-related risks. In particular, we need to educate our patients better about the various medications that we so frequently utilize. Transparency, openness, and increased self-disclosure can all contribute to enhanced treatment outcomes, patient-doctor relationships, and improved health care efficacy.

Dr. Forrest has written an excellent book about a very basic but also extremely important and relevant topic in psychiatry and psychotherapy. Unfortunately, this topic is so basic and seemingly simple that it is often overlooked by clinicians. Psychiatrists and physicians will benefit from reading this text.

Robert A., M.D.

Therapist self-disclosure can be useful in the field of counseling, but I find it unfortunate that most counselors really don't have much of anything to disclose of interest. I work with a lot of young people and people who are entering the addictions counseling field. It seems that the people who come into the field who have completed their recoveries very earnestly want to share and disclose their experiences. The fact is that they can do that at any AA meeting. Many somehow think that people will be interested in how disturbed they have been. Now they are not disturbed or actively addicted, and this makes a great story. However, their stories have just begun. Personal disclosures in addictions and recoveries have been overdone. Entering the field of chemical dependency counseling from personal recovery only continues the fascination with the world you were trying to escape from. And that world is definitely not fascinating! Quite frankly, if it was as fascinating as some counselors make it out to be, there would be money in it! People would pay counselors to hear their stories and disclosures.

I think most people who go into the chemical dependency counseling field as a result of their personal addictions or recoveries seldom have lives worth a dime's worth of interest. So what are they going to disclose? Would it really be interesting to hear a guy tell a therapist, "Geez doc, I had a fight with my wife last night." And the therapist might respond, "Geez, just last week I had a Kodiak bear try to rip my heart out." Would this be construed as a therapeutic disclosure in the counseling relationship or a very interesting life event?

For years, counselors have focused on the effects of counselor disclosure. Instead of counselor's saying, "It must have been very difficult fighting your wife," it would be refreshing to hear the counselor disclose, "Christ, you've been fighting with the same woman for years. Why don't you get the hell out of that relationship and take a trip to the Caribbean or Mexico for a month." Or "Doesn't this get a little old? I mean it's really getting old for me just listening to you, and it must be really tedious to live with." Or, "Living a life in an ineffectual manner sounds duller than a box of dirt." Counselor disclosures such as these are direct and a lot of times just rigorously honest.

I think attempting to help foster change in people's lives demands that therapists have at least a life of interest. Growing petunias doesn't cut it. Counselors might be better served climbing Denali, visiting Africa, and learning the autoharp. Living a life of empathy and self-disclosure would certainly put a crimp in self-definition. I am not sure being able to try and understand what a deviant thinks and feels is all that good of a thing, and I'm also reluctant to encourage counselors to openly disclose their deviance to clients or others. Self-disclosure may help clients to talk about themselves more openly, but what do client or counselor disclosures leave you with at the end of the hour?

It seems to me if counselors are to represent the social norm, it would behoove them to represent the best as opposed to what exists at zero on the social continuum. Society employs counselors to keep clients that are working at a community deficit to at least get back to two or three.

Why is it that some therapists are so afraid of self-disclosing? Debate at a recent staff meeting I attended was focused around whether to put our last names on our company name tag. Several counselors feared that some of our clients might hunt us down for whatever reason. There is a lot of comfort in being anonymous and disclosing nothing about yourself. But, if you don't have the stones to put your name on your work, why are you here? If we are to be the artists of the addictions counseling field, then why can't we stand by our work and disclose our innermost thoughts and being? If this is ever going to be a noble profession, counselors need to be proud of what they do and more open to disclosing about many issues.

In the end, we may want to protect ourselves from what the evil men may do to us, but chemical dependency counseling is a high-risk profession, and if we are not ready to disclose everything then how can we stand behind our name, much less the artistry of our work? As the reader may discern, in the end I am ambivalent about self-disclosure in professional counseling relationships.

Tux, CAC III

Traditionally, psychotherapists have been viewed as "people experts," the teachers of life and relationships. They are generally resilient people who have taught the less-resilient how to deal with and survive life's trials and tribulations. The eighties saw a plethora of support groups form for family members of alcoholics and drug addicts, compulsive eaters, gamblers, and sexually promiscuous people. The nineties brought the positive psychology movement with retreats focused on creating happiness and developing positive thinking. Now psychotherapists help survivors of trauma and abuse learn to survive and thrive in the midst of pain and suffering.

Reflective of the American societal viewpoint and within the context of our medical care system, sick people go to see well people who apply treatments to heal them. Treatment is applied to the person—like a cold compress on a swollen appendage. In this conceptual framework, therapist self-disclosure has been about knocking oneself off the pedestal and becoming a real person so as to offset the power differential between the therapist and patient and facilitate client self-disclosure and trust. With self-disclosure, patients can see their healers as real persons and can develop feeling toward their doctor/psychotherapist, which generalize toward other people in their real lives. Patients may strengthen their motivation to change through their therapist's self-disclosures, which contributes to a stronger therapeutic connection.

As a psychotherapist ever on the search for skills to help people, I use personal stories and life struggles as ways to affectively awaken people and intellectually stimulate cognitive shifts. I have found the most effective forms of self-disclosure to be current hardships (e.g. my father just died) and past hardships (e.g. I quit smoking) mastered.

Self-disclosing a present hardship can be a useful modeling tool for patients, who can then observe the therapist transversing through life's passages and place the therapeutic relationship in "real time." This "real time" perspective aids the therapist in being more present and available to patients, as it allows the therapist to clear his or her mind when there are obvious distractions. In this circumstance, self-disclosure also serves the patient in that patients sense the mood states of the therapist and, left to their own musings, can easily misinterpret or personalize a transient mood state that is an obvious deviation from what is normally present in the therapist.

Sharing stories of past hardships that have been mastered or significantly resolved can serve to instill hope and facilitate growth in patients through encouraging the endurance to effect difficult change through to resolution.

Mindful of therapeutic boundaries, I have used my personal life stories very selectively and rarely, whether they are personal real time events or past hardships transversed. Over the years, I have used self-disclosure within the context of storytelling in general, and most always tell stories that are really composites of people's lives. I often tell stories about other patients I've had, very careful to tell composite stories and change identities like age or gender. I have found it is the storytelling with a function and purpose that has the power to effect change more than it is about disclosing my personal self.

The motive of a self-disclosure by a therapist to a patient is always critical, and the most significant factor for consideration. Is the therapist's core motive altruistic or self-serving? Discernment requires therapist self-awareness and honesty in addition to knowledge about countertransference. Sharing something personal, for instance, "my father recently died," could be told for the message "pain happens to happy people," or "everyone has life tragedies," or "life goes on amidst the tragedies." The disclosure "my father recently died" can also be told for personal gain. It may serve to assuage therapist's guilt or to make an excuse for a lack in performance, e.g. "that's why I've been gone and unable to see my patients" or "that's why I'm distracted as you talk about your problems." Being aware of one's motives is a minute-by-minute, hour-by-hour, day-by-day task of every therapist. It has been referred to as part of the "*art* of psychotherapy" because it is difficult to observe and train therapists in these skills.

We, as therapists, and society at large, abhor the self-serving motivation and actions of a doctor or therapist who uses the power of the therapeutic relationship for personal gain or sexual gratification, yet that gratification is one variation from the theme of therapist orientation attention derived from a self-serving motivation for self-disclosure.

The skill of therapist self-disclosure is about the choice of themes for storytelling and the ability of the therapist to use voice and language to capture the attention and interest of the patient—to create a view previously unseen, ignite a spark of hope, open a door, illuminate a path, and turn on a light.

In the current view of the nature of therapeutic relationships, therapists possess strategies and protocols for promoting change within people who have the potential to heal themselves, and have their own goals and desires, but lack the strategies or skills to achieve their goals and remove blocks to goal achievement.

The therapist is a resource finder, a strategic designer, and an engineer of change. The goals of therapy are established within the therapeutic relationship as well as the client's goals pertaining to desired change. Storytelling and analogy weave universal truths or cognitive shifts into a patient's perspective—a deviation from the repetitive negative self-referencing beliefs that have been activated and which block new behaviors and desired goals.

It is important to consider these strategies as tools for facilitating change. I still self-disclose to patients, but I don't consider if to be as important a tool as I once did when I was less experienced. To facilitate rapport and build trust, I now focus more on being fully present with my patients and demonstrating unconditional positive regard as I go about my therapeutic work.

Jan Schaad, BA, LCSW

As a graduate student in clinical psychology (PSY.D. program, second year), I'm generally uncomfortable with disclosing about myself with patients. Aside from the therapist disclosure and information sheet that we give to clients during their first session, I've pretty much been taught to avoid disclosing anything personal to my clients. We have discussed self-disclosure in one or two of my graduate classes (theories of counseling and psychotherapy), but my practician supervisors have all cautioned us about the potential risks and transference issues that can be related to therapist self-disclosure with their patients. But we've also learned that therapist self-disclosure can be constructive and essential to helping many patients at different stages in therapy. I think it's also important to point out that I'm in a cognitive-behavioral oriented training program, and our faculty and clinician supervisors have all been trained in rational-emotive or cognitive-behavioral oriented programs too. We've learned that appropriate and effective therapist self-disclosures take place more often in the domain of more experienced and older therapists.

I generally believe that I am limited by my lack of professional experience and training to utilize self-disclosure.s in my current therapeutic work, but I also believe that I will be much more skilled and comfortable using this therapeutic technique or tool in my future therapeutic relationships. I also know that I've become much more open and self-disclosing with my fellow students and our department faculty over the past few years, and I'm a better person and student and less anxious as a result of these changes! I'm realizing as I write this short article that I've become a much more open and self-disclosing person as a result of my graduate school education and training. In this regard, I also feel that my increased capacity for self-disclosure has been a very constructive personal growth process.

Sharon Z, MA, PSY. D. (CAND)

SUMMARY

A diversity of client and therapist perspectives about self-disclosure in therapeutic and helping relationships were presented in this chapter. All of these viewpoints are based upon the various experiences of the contributors.

The recovering contributors to this chapter openly stressed the importance and positive impact of self-disclosure on their lives and recovery process. Most of these contributors reported that they had learned to be more open and disclosing as a result of their professional treatment experiences and self-help (AA, NA, etc.) involvements. They also tended to perceive the self-disclosing behaviors of their counselors and therapists as helpful and constructively therapeutic in nature. It is significant that virtually all of the recovering contributors emphasized the importance of becoming progressively more honest in their self-disclosures. These individuals noted that they developed the capacity to be more open and honestly disclosing as they sustained substance abstinence and continued to be active in counseling as well as actively engaged in self-help recovery programs. These reflections seem to imply that self-disclosure alone is simply not enough. Continued drug abstinence and more global personality growth and change in therapy and the recovery process occurs as a part of the recovering person's evolving capacity to become both more disclosing and more honest or forthright in his or her self-disclosing behaviors. I would suspect that the depth and personal scope of the recovering person's self-disclosures also change with sustained recovery and ongoing therapeutic work.

Therapist contributors to the chapter seem to generally agree that their personal self-disclosing behaviors as well as client self-disclosures are important ingredients in therapeutic relationships. However, these contributors also consensually acknowledge that therapist self-disclosure is only one of many core ingredients in effective therapeutic relationships.

Each contributor also personally discloses how professional training and education as well as actual therapeutic experiences have impacted and shaped his or her viewpoints and uses of personal self-disclosure in psychotherapy and addictions counseling. All seem to be generally cognizant of the relative risks, rewards, ethical considerations, timing, and potential therapeutic benefits associated with the uses and abuses of therapist self-disclosure in treatment relationships. It is interesting that the contributors also differ in their viewpoints and personal utilization of self-disclosures in therapy. For example, Doctor A. reports that he has become more self-disclosing in his relationships with patients over the years while Jan indicated that she uses fewer self-disclosures and perceives self-disclosure as less important after many years of therapeutic experience. Tux reports that the self-disclosures of most chemical dependency counselors are simply uninteresting and "overdone" in addiction treatment and recovery work.

Finally, I want to disclose some of my most basic beliefs and thoughts about self-disclosure in psychotherapy and recovery. As a young doctoral student I was greatly impacted by the work of Sid Jourard, and he actually contributed to my first doctoral dissertation at the University of North Dakota. Needless to say, I had very little clinical experience with actual psychotherapy clients and no clinical experience with alcoholics and substance abusers at that time. However, I had previously completed a six month master's level internship with Dr. Charles B. Truax at the Hot Springs Rehabilitation, Research and Training Center (Hot Springs, Arizona, via the University of Missouri, Columbia) and became academically convinced of the therapeutic importance and efficacy of therapist-offered consistent high levels of nonpossessive warmth, empathy, genuineness (self-disclosure), and concreteness within the context of psychotherapy and counseling relationships with virtually all patients or client populations.

For the past forty-two years I have spent over 80 percent of my professional career doing counseling and psychotherapy work with several thousand late adolescent and adult patients. Most of my patients or clients over the past thirty-seven years have been alcoholics and people who manifested a diversity of very severe addictions or substance use disorders. Based upon my extensive clinical experiences over all these years, I am far more convinced than I ever was as a graduate student or neophyte therapist of the powerful therapeutic impact and very complex roles that both therapist and client self-disclosures play within the context of psychotherapy as well as all other human relationships.

In sum, it has been my consistent clinical experience over all these years of therapeutic work that therapist and client self-disclosing behaviors unendingly impact the therapeutic relationship in a multiplicity of complex and nefarious ways. Furthermore, client and therapist self-disclosures consistently benefit and enhance therapeutic relationships and outcomes.

Bibliography

Ackerman, N. (1954). Interpersonal disturbances in the family: Some unsolved problems in psychotherapy. In: Erickson, G.D. and Hogan, T.P. (Eds.). *Family therapy: An introduction to theory and technique.* New York: Jason Aronson, Inc.

Adams, A. J. (2009). *Undrunk.* Center City, MN: Hazelden.

Alcoholics Anonymous (1939). New York: Alcoholics Anonymous World Services, Inc.

Alexander, F. M. (1956). *Psychoanalysis and psychotherapy.* New York: W.W. Norton.

American Psychological Association. (1992). Ethical principles of psychologists and code of conduct. *American Psychologist,* 47, 1597–1611.

Barkham, M., and Shapiro, D. A. (1986). Counselor verbal response modes and experienced empathy. *Journal of Counseling Psychology,* 33, 3–10.

Barrett, M. S., and Berman, J. S. (2001). Is psychotherapy more effective when therapists disclose information about themselves? *Journal of Consulting and Clinical Psychology,* 69, 597–609.

Bateson, G., Jackson, D. D., Haley, J., and Weakland, J. (1956). Toward a theory of schizophrenia. *Behavioral Science,* 1: 251–264.

Behnke, S. (2007). Disclosures of information: Thoughts on a process. *Monitor on Psychology,* 38 (4), 62–63.

———. (2005). On being an ethical psychologist. American Psychological Association, *Monitor on psychology,* 36 (7), 114–115.

Black, C. (1981). *It will never happen to me.* Denver, MAC Publisher, CO.

Blane, H. T. (1968). *The personality of the alcoholic.* New York: Harper and Row.

Blane, H.T., and Leonard, K.E. (Eds.) (1987). *Psychological theories of drinking and alcoholism.* New York: The Guilford Press.

Bonitz, V. (2008). Use of physical touch in the "talking cure": A journey to the outskirts of psychotherapy. *Psychology: Theory, Research, Practice and Training,* 45 (3), 391–403.

Boriskin, J. A. (2009). Understanding, assessing and treating complex PTSD. Presented at Psychotherapy Associates, P.C. 35th annual international "Addictive Disorders and Behavioral Health" Winter Symposium, January 29, Colorado Springs, CO.

Bowen, M. (1978). Family therapy in clinical practice. New York: Jason Aronson, Inc.

Bram, A. D. (1995). The physically ill or dying psychotherapist: A review of ethical and clinical considerations. *Psychotherapy,* 32, 568–580.

Bratter, T. E., and Forrest, G. G. (Eds) (1985). *Alcoholism and substance abuse: Strategies for clinical intervention.* New York: Free Press.

Bridges, N. A. (2001). Therapist's self-disclosure: Expanding the comfort zone. *Psychotherapy: Theory, Research, Practice and Training,* 38 (1), 21–30.

Brown, L. S. (2004). Feminist paradigms of trauma treatment. *Psychotherapy: Theory, Research, Practice and Training,* 41 (4), 464–471.

———. (1994). *Subversive dialogues: Theory in feminist therapy.* New York: Basic Books.

Brown, L. S., and Walker, L. E. (1990). Feminist therapy perspectives on self-disclosure. In G. Stricker and M. Fisher (Eds.), *Self-disclosure in the therapeutic relationship* (135–136). New York: Plenum.

Bruni, C. (2006). Recovery: Thriving in work and school. *Schizophrenia Digest,* Spring, 50–51. New York: Buffalo.

Bugenthal, J. F. T. (1996). *The search for authenticity.* New York: Holt, Rinehart and Winston.

Burlingame, G. M., Fuhriman, A., and Johnson, J. E. (2001). Cohesion in group psychotherapy. *Psychotherapy: Theory, Research, Practice and Training,* 38 (4), 373–379.

Cashwell, C. S., Shcherbakova, J., and Cashwell, T. H. (2003). Effect of client and counselors ethnicity on preference for counselor disclosure. *Journal of Counseling and Development,* 81 (2), 196–201.

Cepeda, L. M., and Davenport, D. S. (2006). Person-centered therapy and solution-focused brief therapy: An integration of present and future awareness. *Psychotherapy: Theory, Research, Practice and Training,* 43 (1), 1–12.

Cherbosque, J. (1987). Differential effects of counselor self-disclosure statements on perception of the counselor and willingness to disclose: A cross-cultural study. *Psychotherapy,* 24, 434–437.

Cook, J. M., Biyanova, T., and Coyne, J. C. (2009). Influential psychotherapy figures, authors, and books: An internet survey of over 2,000 psychotherapists. *Psychotherapy: Theory, Research, Practice and Training,* 46 (1), 42–51.

Cooper, S. (1998). Analyst subjectivity, analyst disclosure, and the aims of psychoanalysis. *Psychoanalytic Quarterly,* LXVII, 379–400.

Counselman, E. F. (197). Self-disclosure, tears, and the dying client. *Psychotherapy: Theory, Research, Practice and Training,* 34 (3), 233–237.

Curtis, L. L., and Hodge, M. (1994). Old standards, new dilemmas: Ethics and boundaries in community support services. *Psychosocial Rehabilitation Journal,* 18, 13–33.

Dalenberg, C. J. (2004). Maintaining the safe and effective therapeutic relationship in the context of distrust and anger: Countertransference and complex trauma. *Psychotherapy: Theory, Research, Practice and Training,* 14 (4), 438–447.

De Quardo, J. (2006). Schizophrenia update. Presented at Psychotherapy Associates, P.C. 32nd annual international "Addictive Disorders and Behavioral Health" Winter Symposium, January 25, Colorado Springs, CO.

DeForest, C. ,and Stone, G. L. (1980). Effects of sex and intimacy level on self-disclosure. *Journal of Counseling Psychology,* 27, 93–96.

Dillon, D. (2006). Crystal balling future trends in addiction and behavioral medicine. Presented at Psychotherapy Associates, P.C. 32nd annual international "Addictive Disorders and Behavioral Health" Winter Symposium, January 27, Colorado Springs, CO.

Dove, W. R. (1995). Ethics training for the alcohol/drug abuse professional. *Alcohol Treatment Quarterly,* 12 (4), 19–30.

Dowd, E. T., and Boroto, D. R. (1982). Differential effects of counselor self-disclosure, self-involving statements, and interpretation. *Journal of Counseling Psychology,* 29, 8–13.

Dryden, W. (1990). Self-disclosure in rational-emotive therapy. In G. Stricker and M. Fisher (Eds.), *Self-disclosure in the therapeutic relationship* (pp. 61–74). New York: Plenum.

Dunn, E. C., Neighbors, C., and Larimer, M. E. (2006). Motivational enhancement therapy and self-help treatment for binge eaters. *Psychology of Addictive Behaviors,* 20 (1), 44–52.

Edwards, C. E., and Murdock, N. L. (1994). Characteristics of therapist self-disclosure in the counseling process. *Journal of Counseling and Development,* 72, 384–389.

Ellis, A. (1996). Reason and emotion in psychotherapy. New York: Carol Publishing Group.

Epstein, R. S. (1994). *Keeping boundaries: Maintaining safety and integrity in the psychotherapeutic process.* Washington, D.C.: American Psychiatric Press.

Eysenck, H. J. (1965). The effects of psychotherapy. *International Journal of Psychiatry,* 1, 97–178.

Farber, B. A. (2006). *Self-disclosure in psychotherapy.* New York: Guilford Press.

Farber, B. A., Khurgin-Bott, R., and Feldman, S. (2009). The benefits and risks of-patient self-disclosure in psychotherapy of women with a history of childhood sexual abuse. *Psychotherapy: Theory, Research, Practice and Training,* 46 (1), 52–67.

Farber, B. A., and Sohn, A. E. (2007). Patterns of self-disclosure in psychotherapy and marriage. *Psychotherapy: Theory, Research, Practice, and Training,* 44 (2), 226–231.

Fenichel, O. (1945). *The psychoanalytic theory of neurosis.* New York: W.W. Norton.

Ferenezi, S. (1950/1919). On the techniques of psychoanalysis. *Further contributions to the theory and techniques of psycho-analysis* (pp. 177–189). London: Hogarth Press.

Fleiss, R. (1942). The metapsychology of the analyst. *Psychoanalytic Quarterly,* 1, 211–227.

Fleming, J. L. (2009). Bipolar disorder, major psychiatric disorders and substance abuse: Treatment update. Presented at Psychotherapy Associates, P. C. 35th annual international "Addictive Disorders and Behavioral Health" Winter Symposium, January 30, Colorado Springs, CO.

———. (2008). New and innovative treatments for bipolar disorder, depression and substance abuse. Presented at Psychotherapy Associates, P.C. 34th annual international "Addictive Disorders and Behavioral Health" Winter Symposium, January 30, Colorado Springs, CO.

Forrest, G. G. (2009). Alcohol dependence and alcohol use disorders: Etiology, differential diagnosis and treatments. Presented at Psychotherapy Associates, P. C. 35th annual international "Addictive Disorders and Behavioral Health" Winter Symposium, January 28, Colorado Springs, CO.

———. (2008). Training, supervising and mentoring chemical dependency counselors. Presented at Psychotherapy Associates, P.C. 34th annual international "Addictive Disorders and Behavioral Health" Winter Symposium, February 1, Colorado Springs, CO.

———. (2007). Intensive psychotherapy of alcoholism: Reflections on 35 years of clinical practice and 10,000 patients. Presented at Psychotherapy Associates, P.C. 33rd annual international "Addictive Disorders and Behavioral Health" Winter Symposium, January 30, Colorado Springs, CO.

———. (2006). Drinking disorders: Etiology, assessment and treatment. Presented at Psychotherapy Associates, P.C., 32nd Annual International "Addictive Disorders and Behavioral Health" Winter Symposium, January 24, Colorado Springs, CO.

———. (2005). Psychotherapy and assessment of substance use disorders. Presented at Psychotherapy Associates, P.C. 31st Annual International "Addictive Disorders and Behavioral Health" Winter Symposium, January 25, Colorado Springs, CO.

———. (2002). *Countertransference in chemical dependency counseling.* Binghamton, NY: The Haworth Press, Inc.

———. (2001). *How to live with a problem drinker and survive* (rev. 2nd ed). Holmes Beach, FL: Learning Publications, Inc.

———. (1999). *Alcoholism, narcissism and psychopathology.* New York: Jason Aronson, Inc .

———. (1997). *Intensive psychotherapy of alcoholism.* New York: Jason Aronson, Inc.

———. (1995). *Chemical dependency and antisocial personality disorder: Psychotherapy and assessment strategies.* Binghamton, New York: The Haworth Press.

———. (1994). *The diagnosis and treatment of alcoholism* (2nd ed.). New York: Jason Aronson, Inc.

———. (1992). *Confrontation in psychotherapy with the alcoholic* (2nd ed.). Holmes Beach, FL: Learning Publications, Inc.

———. (1991). Role slippage and adaptation in the alcoholic family system. *Family Dynamics of Addiction Quarterly,* 1 (3), 315–339.

———. (1984). Psychotherapy of alcoholics and substance abusers: Outcome assessment revisited. *Family and Community Health,* 2 (1), 40–50.

———. (1978). *The diagnosis and treatment of alcoholism* (2nd ed.). Springfield, IL: Charles C. Thomas.

——— (1970). Transparency as a prognostic variable in psychotherapy. Unpublished doctoral dissertation. University of Grand Forks, ND.

Freimuth, M. (2008). Another missed opportunity: Recognition of alcohol use problems by mental health providers. *Psychotherapy: Theory, Research, Practice and Training,* 45 (3), 405–409.

Freud, S. (1912/2002). Recommendation to physicians practicing psychoanalysis. *The standard edition of the complete psychological works of Sigmund Freud* (volume 12, pp 111–112).

Fromm-Reichmann, F. (1950). *Principles of intensive psychotherapy.* Chicago: University of Chicago Press.

Fuhriman, A., and Burlingame, G. M. (1994). Group psychotherapy: Research and practice. In A. Fuhriman and G. M. Burlingame (eds.), *Handbook of group psychotherapy: An empirical and clinical synthesis* (pp 3–40). New York: Wiley.

Gabbard, G. O. (1996). Lessons to be learned from the study of sexual boundary violations. *American Journal of Psychotherapy,* 50, 311–322.

Geller, J. D., and Farber, B. A. (1997, August). Why therapists do and don't disclose. Paper presented at the annual meeting of the American Psychological Association, Chicago, IL.

Glasser, W. (2007). Treating addictions as a public health issue: Role playing and clinical demonstrations. Presented at Psychotherapy Associates, P.C. 34th annual international "Addictive Disorders and Behavioral Health" Winter Symposium, February 1, Colorado Springs, CO.

Glasser, W. (2007). Treating addictions as a public health issue. Presented at: Psychotherapy Associates, P.C. 33rd annual international "Addictive Disorders and Behavioral Health" Winter Symposium, January 31, Colorado Springs, CO.

Glasser W. (2005). Reality therapy and choice theory training. Presented at: Psychotherapy Associates, P.C. 31st annual international "Addictive Disorders and Behavioral Health" Winter Symposium, January 28, Colorado Springs, CO.

Glasser, W. (2003). *Warning: Psychiatry can be hazardous to your health.* New York: Harper Collins.

Glasser, W. (2001). *Counseling with choice theory: The new reality therapy.* Harper Collins Publishers, Inc.

Glasser, W. (2000). *Reality therapy in action.* New York: Harper Collins Publishers, Inc.

Glasser, W. (1965). *Reality therapy: A new approach to psychiatry.* New York: Harper and Row Publishers.

Goldstein, E. G. (1997). To tell or not to tell: The disclosure of events in the therapist's life to the patient. *Clinical Social Work Journal,* 25, 41–58.

Goldstein, E. G. (1994). Self-disclosure in treatment: What therapists do and don't talk about. *Clinical Social Work Journal,* 22, 417–433.

Goodman, L. A., Liang, B., Helms, J. E., Latta, R. E., Sparks, E., and Weinstraub, S. R. (2004). Training counseling psychologists as social justice agents: Feminist and multicultural principles in action. *The Counseling Psychologist,* 32 (6), 793–837.

Goodyear, R., and Schumate, J. (1996). Perceived effects of therapist self-disclosure on attraction to clients. *Professional Psychology: Research and Practice,* 27, 613–616.

Greenberg, L. R. (1990). Self-disclosure in psychotherapy: Working with older adults. In G. Stricker and M. Fisher (Eds.), *Self-disclosure in the therapeutic relationship* (pp. 179–190). New York: Plenum.

Gurman, A. S. (1977). The patient's perception of the therapeutic relationship. In: A. S. Gurman and A. M. Razin (Eds.), *Effective psychotherapy: A handbook of research* (pp. 503–543). New York: Pergamon Press.

Gutheil, T. G., and Gabbard, G. O. (1995). The concept of boundaries in clinical practice: Theoretical and risk management decisions. In D. N. Bersoff (Ed.), *Ethical conflicts in psychology* (pp. 218–223). Washington D.C.: American Psychological Association.

Hahn, W. K. (2000). Shame: Countertransference identifications in individual psychotherapy. *Psychotherapy: Theory, Research, Practice and Training,* 37 (1), 10–21.

Halbur, D. A., and Halbur, K. V. (2006). *Developing your theoretical orientation in counseling and psychotherapy.* Boston: Pearson, Allyn and Bacon.

Haley, J. (1959). The family of the schizophrenic: A model system. In: Erickson, G. D. and Hogan, T. P. (eds.). *Family Therapy: An introduction to therapy and technique.* New York: Jason Aronson, Inc.

Haley, J. (1963). Marriage therapy. *Archives of General Psychiatry,* 8: 213–224.

Hartung, J., and Galvin, M. (2003). *Energy psychology and EMDR.* New York: Norton.

Hawkins, I. L., and Bullock, S. L. (1995). Informed consent and religious values: A neglected area of diversity. *Psychotherapy,* 32, 293–300.

Hill, C. E., Helms, J. E., Tichenor, V., Spiegel, S. B., O'Grady, K. E., and Perry, E. S. (1988). The effects of therapist response modes in brief psychotherapy. *Journal of Counseling Psychology,* 35, 222–233.

Hill, C. A., and Knox, S. (2001). Self-disclosure. *Psychotherapy: Theory, Research, Practice and Training,* 38 (4), 413–417.

Hill, C. E., and Lent, R. W. (2006). A narrative and meta-analytic review of helping skills training: Time to revive a dormant area of inquiry. *Psychotherapy: Theory, Research, Practice and Training,* 43 (2), 154–172.

Hill, C. E., Mahalik, J. R., and Thompson, B. J. (1989). Therapist self-disclosure. *Psychotherapy,* 26, 290–295.

Hill, C. E., Stahl, J., and Roffman, M. (2007). Training novice psychotherapists: Helping skills and beyond. *Psychotherapy: Theory Research, Practice and Training,* 44 (4), 364–370.

Hill, C. E., Thames, T. B., and Rardin, D. (1979). A comparison of Rogers, Perls, and Ellis on the Hill Counselor Verbal Response Category System. *Journal of Counseling Psychology,* 26, 198–203.

Hountras, P. T., and Forrest, G. G. (1970). Personality characteristics and self-disclosure in a psychiatric outpatient population. College of Education Record. University of North Dakota, 55: 206–213.

Hymer, S. (1988). *Confessions in psychotherapy.* New York: Gardner Press, Inc.

Jameson, P., Stadter, M., and Poulton, J. (2007). Sustained and Sustaining Continuing Education for Therapists. *Psychotherapy: Theory, Research, Practice and Training,* 44 (1), 110–114.

Jewitt, T. L. (2007). Electro convulsive therapy in psychiatric disorders. Presented at Psychotherapy Associates, P.C. 33rd annual international "Addictive Disorders and Behavioral Health" winter symposium, February 1, Colorado Springs, CO.

Jourard, S. M. (1971). *Self-disclosure: An experienced analysis of the transparent self.* New York: Wiley.

Jourard, S. M. (1968). *Disclosing man to himself.* Princeton, NJ: Van Nostrand.

Jourard, S. M. (1968). Self-disclosure and other cathexis. *Journal of Abnormal and Social Psychology,* 59, 428–431.

Jourard, S. M. (1964). *The transparent self.* Princeton, NJ: Van Nostrand.

Jourard, S. M., and Lasakow, P. (1958). Some factors in self-disclosures. *Journal of Abnormal and Social Psychology,* 56, 91–98.

Kahn, J. H., Vogel, D. L., Schneider, W. J., Barr, L. K., and Herrell, K. (2008). The emotional content of client disclosures and session impact: An analogue study. *Psychotherapy: Theory, Research, Practice and Training,* 45 (4), 539–545.

Kasper, L. B., Hill, C. E., and Kirlighan, Jr., D. M. (2008). Therapist immediacy in brief psychotherapy: Case study I. *Psychotherapy: Theory, Research, Practice and Training,* 45 (3), 281–297.

Kernberg, O. F. (1975). *Borderline conditions and pathological narcissism.* New York: Jason Aronson, Inc.

Kirschenbaum, H., and Jourdan, A. (2005). The current status of Carl Rogers and the person-centered approach. *Psychotherapy: Theory, Research, Practice and Training,* 42 (1), 37–51.

Kitchener, K. (1986). Teaching applied ethics in counselor education: An integration of psychological processes and philosophical analysis. *Journal of Counseling and Development,* 64, 306–310.

Klein, D. N., Shwartz, J. E., Santiago, N. J., Vivian, D., et al. (2003). Therapeutic alliance in depression treatment: Controlling for prior change and patient characteristics. *Journal of Consulting and Clinical Psychology,* 71(6), 997–1006.

Klein, M. H., Kolden, G. G., Michels, J. L., and Chisholm-Stockard, S. (2002). Congruence of genuineness. *Psychotherapy: Theory, Research, Practice and Training,* 38 (4), 396–400.

Knox, S., Hess, S., Petersen, D., and Hill, C. E. (1997). A qualitative analysis of client perceptions of the effects of helpful therapist self-disclosure in long-term therapy. *Journal of Counseling Psychology,* 44, 274–283.

Koocher, G. P., and Keith-Spiegel, P. (1998). *Ethics in psychology: Professional standards and cases* (2nd ed.). New York: Oxford University Press.

Kooden, H. (1991). Self-disclosure: The gay male therapist as agent of social change. In C. Silverstein (Ed.), *Gays, lesbians, and their therapists* (pp. 143–154). New York: Norton.

Kotter, J. A. (1990). *On being a therapist.* San Francisco, CA: Jossey-Bass.

Lambert, M. J. (1992). Psychotherapy outcome research: Implications for integrative and electic therapists. In: J. C. Norcross and M. R. Goldfried (Eds.) *Handbook of psychotherapy integration* (pp. 94–129). New York: Basic Books.

Lane, D. K. (2006). Avoiding malpractice: Best practices for forensic evaluations, responding to critical incidents and record keeping. Presented at Psychotherapy Associates, P.C. and co-sponsors 32nd annual international "Addictive Disorders and Behavioral Health" Winter Symposium, January 26, Colorado Springs, CO.

Lane, D. K., Jr. (2006). *The legal guide to practicing psychotherapy in Colorado.* Denver, CO: Bradford Publishing Co.

Lejuez, C. W., Hopko, D. R., Levine, S., Gholkar, R., and Collins, L. M. (2005). The therapeutic alliance in behavior therapy. *Psychotherapy: Theory, Research, Practice and Training,* 42 (1), 456–468.

Littrell, J. M. (1998). *Brief counseling in action.* New York: W.W. Norton and Co.

Macphee, B. (2004). Double trouble. *Schizophrenia Digest.* Winter, 9. New York: Buffalo.

Mahalik, J. R., Van Ormer, E. A., and Simi, N. L. (2002). Ethical issues in using self-disclosure in feminist therapy. In M. M. Brabeck (Ed.), *Practicing feminist ethics in psychology* (pp. 189–201). Washington DC: American Psychological Association.

Mallinckrodt, B., Porter, M. J., and Kivlighan, D. M., Jr. (2005). Client attachment to therapist, depth of in-session exploration, and object relations in brief psychotherapy. *Psychotherapy: Theory, Research, Practice and Training,* 42 (1), 85–100.

Maroda, K. (1991). *The power of countertransference.* New York: John Wiley.

Maroda, K. (1994). *The power of countertransference: Innovations in analytic technique:* Northvale, NJ: Jason Aronson, Inc.

Maroda, K. (1999). Creating an intersubjective context of self-disclosure. *Smith College Studies in Social Work,* 69 (2), 475–489.

Miller, W. R., and Rollnick, S. (2002). *Motivational interviewing: Preparing people for change* (2nd ed.). New York: Guilford Press.

Minuchin, S. (1965). Conflict-resolution family therapy. In: Erickson, G.D. and Hogan, T.P. (Eds.). *Family therapy: An introduction to therapy and technique.* New York: Jason Aronson, Inc.

Mowrer, O. H. (1961). Psychopathology and the problem of guilt, confession and expiation. In: W. Dennis (Ed.), *Current trends in psychological theory* (pp. 208–229). Pittsburgh: University of Pittsburgh Press.

Mowrer, O. H. (1964). *The new group therapy.* Princeton, N.J.: Van Nostrand.

Muller, R. T. (2009). Trauma and dismissing (avoidant) attachment: Intervention strategies in individual psychotherapy: *Psychotherapy: Theory, Research, Practice and Training,* 46 (1), 68–81.

Myers, D, and Hayes J. A. (2006). Effects of therapist general self-disclosure and countertransference disclosure on ratings of the therapist session. *Psychotherapy: Theory, Research and Training,* 43 (2), 173–185.

Neimeyer, G. J., and Fong, M. L. (1983). Self-disclosure flexibility and counselor effectiveness. *Journal of Counseling Psychology,* 30, 258–261.

Norcross, J. C. (Ed.) (2002). *Psychotherapy relationships that work: Therapist contributions and responsiveness to patients.* New York: Oxford University Press.

Norcross, J. C., Bike, D. H., and Evans, K. L. (2009). The therapist's therapist: A replication and extension 20 years later. *Psychotherapy: Theory, Research, Practice and Training,* 46 (1) 32–41.

Ogborne, A. C., and Glaser, F. B. (1985). Evaluating alcoholics anonymous. In Bratter, T.E. and Forrest, G.G. (Eds.), *Alcoholism and substance abuse: Strategies for clinical intervention.* New York: The Free Press.

Paolino, T. J., and McCrady, B. S. (1977). *The alcoholic marriage: Alternative perspectives.* New York: Grune and Stratton.

Papouchis, N. (1990). Self-disclosure and psychotherapy with children and adolescents. In G. Stricker and M. Fisher (eds.), *Self-disclosure in the therapeutic relationship* (pp. 157–174). New York: Plenum.

Patterson, C. H. (1966). *Theories of counseling and psychotherapy.* New York: Harper and Row, Publishers.

Pearls, F. S. (1969). *Gestalt therapy verbatim.* Lafayette, CA: Real People Press.

Peca-Baker, T. A., and Frielander, M. L. (1987). Effects of role expectations on client's perceptions of disclosing and nondisclosing counselors. *Journal of Counseling and Development,* 66, 78–81.

Perlman, G. (1991). The question of therapist self-disclosure in the treatment of a married gay man. In C. Silverstein (Ed.), *Gays, lesbians, and their therapists* (pp. 143–154). New York: Norton.

Perrin, D. K., and Dowd, E. T. (1986). Effect of paradoxical and nonparadoxical self-disclosure on counselor social influence. *Journal of Counseling Psychology,* 33, 207–210.

Peterson, Z. D. (2002). More than a mirror: The ethics of therapist self-disclosure. *Psychotherapy: Theory, Research, Practice and Training,* 39 (1) 21–31.

Ponterotto, J. G., Casas, J. M., Suzuki, L. A., and Alexander, C. M. (1995). *Handbook of multicultural counseling.* Thousand Oaks, CA: Sage.

Reik, T. (1948). *Listening with the third ear.* New York: Farrar, Strauss, and Young.

Roberts, S. (2004). Dual diagnosis: Substance abuse and schizophrenia equals double trouble. *Schizophrenia Digest.* Winter, 31–36. New York: Buffalo.

Robitschek, C. G., and McCarthy, P. R. (1991). Prevalence of counselor self-reference in the therapeutic dyad. *Journal of Counseling and Development,* 69, 218–221.

Roes, N. A. (2004). The rules of self-disclosure. *Counselor,* 5 (6), 26–28.

Rogers, C. R. (1942). *Counseling and psychotherapy: New Concepts in practice.* Boston: Houghton Mifflin.

Rogers, C. R. (1961). *On becoming a person.* Boston: Houghton Mifflin.

Rogers, C. R. (1958). The characteristics of a helping relationship. *Personnel and Guidance Journal,* 37, 6–16.

Rogers, C. R. (1957). The necessary and sufficient conditions of psychotherapeutic personality change. *Journal of Consulting Psychology,* 21 (2), 95–103.

Rogers, C. R. (1951). *Client-centered therapy: Its current practice.* Boston: Houghton Mifflin.

Rogers, C. R., and Dymond, R. (Eds.) (1954). *Psychotherapy and personality change.* Chicago: University Press.

Ruitenbeck, H. M. (1971). *Group therapy today.* New York: Atherton Press, Inc.

Ruth, R. (2007). Ethics and evidence-based practices: Are we asking the right questions: *The Register Report,* 33 (Spring), 33–39.

Saccuzzo, D., and Johnson, N. E. (2007). What early career psychologists need to know about malpractice liability. *The Register Report,* 33 (Spring), 24–31.

Safran, J. D., and Muran, J. C. (2005). *Negotiating the therapeutic alliance: A relational treatment guide.* New York: Guilford Press.

Satir, V. (1967). *Conjoint family therapy: A guide to theory and technique.* Palo Alto: Science and Behavior Books.

Schaad, J. (2009). EMDR in the treatment of anxiety disorders, PTSD and trauma. Presented at the Psychotherapy Associates, P. C. 35th annual international "Addictive Disorders and Behavioral Health" Winter Symposium, January 30, Colorado Springs, CO.

Schaad, J. (2005). Ethical decision making in mental health and chemical dependency treatment settings. Presented at: Psychotherapy Associates, P.C. 31st annual international "Addictive Disorders and Behavioral Health" Winter Symposium, January 28, Colorado Springs, CO.

Shaffer, H. J. (2006). Toward a syndrome model of addiction. Presented at Psychotherapy Associates, P.C. 32nd annual international "Addictive Disorders and Behavioral Health" Winter Symposium, January 25, Colorado Springs, CO.

Shapiro, F. (2001). *EMDR as an integrative psychotherapy approach* (Ed.). Washington D.C.: American Psychological Association.

Shapiro, F. (2001). *Eye movement de-sensitization and reprocessing* (2nd ed.). New York: Guilford Press.

Simi, N. L., and Mahalik, J. R. (1997). Comparison of feminist versus psychoanalytic/dynamic and other therapists on self-disclosure. *Psychology of Women Quarterly,* 21, 465–483.

Simon, J. C. (1990). Criteria for therapist self-disclosure. In: G. Stricker and M. Fisher (Eds.), *Self-disclosures in the therapeutic relationship* (pp. 207–225). New York: Plenum.

Simone, D. H., McCarthy, P., and Skay, C. L. (1988). An investigation of client and counselor variables that influence likelihood of counselor self-disclosure. *Journal of Counseling and Development,* 76, 174–182.

Skeel, R. L., Pilarski, C., Pytlak, K. and Neudecker, J. (2008). Personality and performance-based measures in the prediction of alcohol use. *Psychology of Addictive Behaviors,* 22 (3), 402–409.

Slakter, E. (1987). Reality issues and countertransference. In E. Slakter (Ed.), *Countertransference* (pp. 219–226). Northvale, NJ: Jason Aronson, Inc.

Slavson, S. R. (1956). *The fields of group psychotherapy.* New York: International Universities Press.

Solomon, M. F., Neborsky, R. J., McCullough, L., Alpert, M., Shapiro, F., and Malan, D. (2001). *Short-term therapy for long-term change.* New York, NY: W.W. Norton & Co.

Stein, J. A., Dixon, E. L., and Nyamathi, A. M. (2008). Effects of psychosocial and situational variables on substance abuse among homeless adults. *Psychology of Addictive Behaviors,* 22 (3), 410–416.

Stiles, W. B., Shapiro, D. A., and Firth-Cozens, J. A. (1988). Do sessions of different treatments have different impacts? *Journal of Counseling Psychology,* 35, 391–396.

Sue, D. W., and Sue, D. (1999). *Counseling the culturally different: Theory and practice* (3rd ed.). New York: Wiley.

Sullivan, H. S. (1953). The interpersonal theory of psychiatry. New York: Norton.

Tansey, M., and Burke, W. (1989). *Understanding countertransference: From projective identification to empathy.* Hillsdale, NJ: Analytic Press.

Teasdale, A. C., and Hill, C. E. (2006). Preferences of therapists-in-training for client characteristics. *Psychotherapy: Theory, Research, Practice and Training,* 43 (1) 111–118.

Tillman, J. G. (1998). Psychodynamic psychotherapy, religious beliefs, and self-disclosure. *American Journal of Psychotherapy,* 52, 273–286.

Truax, C. B., and Carkhuff, R. R. (1967). *Toward effective counseling and psychotherapy.* Chicago: Aldine.

Truax, C. B., and Lister, J. L. (1971). Effects of short-term training upon accurate empathy and nonpossessive warmth. *Counselor Education and Supervision,* 10: 120–125.

Truax, C. B. ,and Mitchell, K. M. (1971). Research on certain therapist interpersonal skills in relation to process and outcome. In: A.E. Bergin and S.L. Garfield (Eds.), *Handbook of psychotherapy and behavior change* (pp. 299–344). New York: Wiley.

Truax, C. B., and Wargo, D. (1966). *Antecedents to outcome in group psychotherapy with juvenile delinquents: Effects of therapeutic conditions, alternate sessions, vicarious therapy, pretraining and patient self-exploration.* An unpublished manuscript. University of Arkansas, Arkansas Rehabilitation Research and Training Center, Hot Springs, AR.

Vamos, M. (1993). The bereaved therapist and her patients. *American Journal of Psychotherapy,* 47, 296–305.

Vogel, D. L., Wester, S. R., and Larson, L. M. (2007). Avoidance of counseling; Psychological factors that inhibit seeking help. *Journal of Counseling and Development,* 85 (4), 410–422.

Wachtel, P. L. (1993). *Therapeutic communication: Principles and effective practice.* New York: Guilford Press.

Wanner, B., Vitaro, F., Carbonneau, R., and Tremblay, R. E. (2009). Cross-lagged links among gambling, substance use, and delinquency from midadolescence to young adulthood: Addictive and moderating effects of common risk factors. *Psychology of Addictive Behaviors,* 23 (1), 91–104.

Watkins, C. E., Jr. (1990). The effects of counselor self-disclosure: A research review. *The Counseling Psychologist,* 18, 477–500.

Wegscheider, S. (1981). *Another Chance: Hope and health for the alcoholic family.* Palo Alto: Science and Behavior Books, Inc.

Wei, M., and Heppner, P. P. (2005). Counselor and client predictions of the initial working alliance: A replication and extension to Taiwanese client-counselor dyads. *The Counseling Psychologist,* 33 (1), 51–71.

Weiner, M. F. (1983). *Therapist disclosure: The use of self in psychotherapy* (2nd ed.). Baltimore: University Park.

Wells, T. (1994). Therapist self-disclosure: Its effects on clients and the treatment relationship. *Smith College Studies in Social Work,* 65, 22–41.

Whitaker, C. (1958). Psychotherapy with couples. *American Journal of Psychotherapy,* 12, pp 18–23.

Wolf, A. (1950). The psychoanalysis of groups. *American Journal of Psychotherapy,* 4, 16–50.

Wubbolding, R. E. (2009). The WDE system of reality therapy in pretreatment, middle and advanced stages of recovery: Practical no-nonsense counseling and therapy. Presented at Psychotherapy Associates, P. C. 35th annual international "Addictive Disorders and Behavioral Health" Winter Symposium, January 31, Colorado Springs, CO.

Yalom, I. (1995). *The theory and practice of group psychotherapy* (3rd ed.). New York: Basic Books, Inc.

Index

About the Author

Gary G. Forrest, Ed.D., Ph.D., is a licensed clinical psychologist in independent practice and executive director of Psychotherapy Associates, PC ,and the Institute for Addictive Behavioral Change in Colorado Springs, Colorado. A nationally recognized speaker, consultant, and educator, Dr. Forrest has treated more than ten thousand alcoholics, substance abusers, and their family members over the past thirty-five years. He is the author of many books on addictions and chemical dependency treatment, including *Countertransference in Chemical Dependency Counseling; Chemical Dependency and Antisocial Personality Disorder: Psychotherapy and Assessment Strategies; Intensive Psychotherapy of Alcoholism; The Diagnosis and Treatment of Alcoholism; How to Live with a Problem Drinker and Survive; Alcoholism, Narcissism and Psychopathology, Substance Abuse, Homicide and Violent Behavior; Alcoholism and Human Sexuality; How to Cope with a Teenage Drinker;* and *Guidelines for Responsible Drinking.*

Dr. Forrest is a member of the American Psychological Association, American Counseling Association, National Register for Health Service Providers in Psychology, and a diplomate in Professional Psychotherapy and Chemical Dependency Counseling, International Academy of Behavioral Medicine, Counseling and Psychotherapy. He has also taught on the graduate and undergraduate faculties of numerous universities and colleges throughout the United States.

www.ingramcontent.com/pod-product-compliance
Ingram Content Group UK Ltd.
Pitfield, Milton Keynes, MK11 3LW, UK
UKHW012041150926
475560UK00001B/134